All the Good

All the Good:

A Wesleyan Way of Christmas

All the Good

978-1-7910-1797-2

978-1-7910-1798-9 eBook

All the Good: Leader Guide

978-1-7910-1800-9

978-1-7910-1801-6 eBook

All the Good: DVD

978-1-7910-1802-3

All the Good: Devotions for the Season

978-1-7910-1809-2

978-1-7910-1810-8 eBook

All the Good

A WESLEYAN WAY
of CHRISTMAS

Laceye Warner • Amy Valdez Barker
Jung Choi • Sangwoo Kim

Abingdon Press | Nashville

All the Good

A Wesleyan Way of Christmas

Copyright © 2021 Abingdon Press
All rights reserved.

Library of Congress Control Number: 2021941506

978-1-7910-1797-2

21 22 23 24 25 26 27 28 29 30 — 10 9 8 7 6 5 4 3 2 1
MANUFACTURED IN THE UNITED STATES OF AMERICA

CONTENTS

About the Authors

Rev. Laceye C. Warner, PhD is Royce and Jane Reynolds Associate Professor of the Practice of Evangelism and Methodist Studies and associate dean for Wesleyan Engagement at Duke University Divinity School. An elder in the Texas Conference, Dr. Warner was appointed to the faculty at Duke Divinity School in 2001. She is the author of several books including *The Method of Our Mission: United Methodist Polity and Organization* (Abingdon Press, 2014) and a contributing editor to the *Wesley Study Bible*. Dr. Warner enjoys living on a flower farm with her family and many of God's creatures.

Rev. Dr. Amy Valdez Barker currently serves as the Visiting Associate Professor of Religious Education and Mission Innovation at Candler School of Theology in Emory University. She has held executive roles at The Connectional Table and Global Ministries of The United Methodist Church. She is an ordained deacon of the North Georgia Annual Conference and a graduate from Garrett-Evangelical Theological Seminary. She has authored a book on trust called *Trust by Design: The Beautiful Behaviors of an Effective Church Culture*. She loves spending time with her two teenage children, her husband, and their Bernedoodle, Gryffin, in their sweet little community of Lilburn, Georgia.

About the Authors

Sangwoo Kim (ThD, Duke) is a consulting professor, senior director of the Methodist House of Studies and the Wesleyan Formation Initiatives, and codirector of Asian House of Studies at Duke Divinity School. He is an elder in the North Carolina Conference of The United Methodist Church, experienced in multicultural and cross-cultural ministries. His academic and pastoral interest includes systematic and liturgical theology, spiritual formation, and Christian prayer.

Jung Choi is a consulting professor, senior director of Wesleyan Formation Initiatives, and codirector of Asian House of Studies at Duke Divinity School. She is a scholar-teacher trained in the New Testament and Early Christianity (MDiv, Harvard; STM, Yale; ThD, Harvard). Before Duke, Choi was an assistant professor of religious studies at North Carolina Wesleyan College, Rocky Mount, NC. She is an instructor for the New Testament courses for the Deaconess and Home Missioners for the United Methodist Women and is working on a textbook on the New Testament. Choi is a Woman of Color Fellow of GBHEM, a John Wesley Fellow with A Foundation of Theological Education (AFTE), and a participant of Wabash Fellowship for Religion Faculty in Asian and Pacific Islander Descent at Wabash Center for Teaching and Learning in Theology and Religion.

Wesleyan Sources

John Wesley's writings are accessible in a number of published resources and web locations. In this study, we draw from the multi-volume work *The Bicentennial Edition of the Works of John Wesley* (Nashville: Abingdon Press, 1976). Documents by John Wesley, including sermons, cited in the study are listed below.

CM	*The Character of a Methodist*
ENNT	*Expository Notes upon the New Testament*
JD	*Journals and Diaries*
PCP	*A Plain Account of Christian Perfection*
PPCM	*A Plain Account of the People Called Methodists*
SCH	Sermon, "Circumcision of the Heart"
SCS	Sermon, "Catholic Spirit"
SNB	Sermon, "New Birth"
SNC	Sermon, "New Creation"
SSWS	Sermon, "Scripture Way of Salvation"
SSM	Sermon, "Sermon on the Mount IV"

Introduction

LACEYE WARNER

The miracle of Advent is the central
belief of Christianity—not that we love God—
but that God loves us.

The season of Advent offers time and space for Christians to prepare for the coming of Jesus Christ at Christmas through reflecting on the story of salvation. Advent begins the Christian liturgical year by not only recounting the birth of Christ but also Jesus Christ's second coming. In Jesus Christ, through the Holy Spirit, God demonstrates God's love for all creation. Jesus is often referred to as Emmanuel, meaning "God is with us" (Matthew 1:23). Through Mary's willingness to carry and care for Jesus, God enters into creation, at the same time fully human and fully divine. Jesus's birth, life, death, and resurrection embody God's unfathomable love for all creation. Advent invites the world to anticipate and receive God's amazing love in Jesus Christ.

In this book, we offer a path to anticipate Jesus Christ's coming through four chapters, each reflecting on biblical texts, Wesleyan themes, and Christian practices. By pondering God's goodness through the Christmas narrative, readers are invited to reflect on and participate in Christian practices, or good works, in response to God's goodness. These practices resemble those encouraged by disciples throughout Christian tradition as well as by the founder of the early Methodist movement, John Wesley.

John Wesley's emphasis on practices of piety and mercy— or good works—drew from the larger Christian tradition. Such practices are often referred to as means of grace. Each chapter guides participants through one of the four weeks of Advent by reflecting on *biblical passages in light of an aspect of Wesleyan means of grace, highlighted by illustrations and stories.* The four chapters respectively describe (1) an overview for preparing the way for God, (2) the impact and significance of prayer, (3) the substance of good works and caring for others, and (4) sharing in God's mission to the world.

"All the Good" of God's Love

When the biblical texts describe God as good, this describes God's actions as well as God's character. Whether in the midst of great joy and celebration or in the midst of deep tragedy, injustice, and natural disasters, God is good because God's love is steadfast. As the liturgical refrain exclaims this biblical theme:

> "God is good all the time
> All the time, God is good."

First and foremost, "All the good" indicates the simple and profound wonder and richness of God's love for all creation.

Biblical texts often refer to the message of God's goodness and love for all as the "good news." Clearly, the message of God's love is not only "good" news, but the most amazing news. In this way, the language of good evokes the depth and texture of God's goodness that surpasses human imagination. The concept of "good news" found in the Gospels is related to the Greek term *euangelizesthai*, meaning "to proclaim good tidings." This term, which appears throughout the Bible, indicates when good tidings from God occurred. It also has a close connection to the announcement of God's salvation in Isaiah, including prominent biblical texts read during Advent.

Related language to "good news" also found throughout the Bible includes *evangelos*, which has as its root *angelos*, "messenger," and *angelo*, "to announce." Significant to understanding these concepts of messenger and announcement is the notion that the message announced is not merely a verbal proclamation of abstract information. Rather, the proclamation of salvation embodies and invites participation in that salvation. The message is a present reality embodied by its messenger that invites a response. Recipients may accept this invitation to participate in the "good news" through Christian practices or good works. The capacity to share the good news of God's love begins with the capacity to receive and embrace God's love and goodness.

What would it mean for us as Christians to understand ourselves as fully loved and accepted by God? What does it mean to accept God's grace in Jesus Christ and live in response to this love and grace? While the following is a simple statement, it is infinitely profound: there is nothing we can do—absolutely nothing—to cause God to love us any more…or any less. For an achievement-driven culture this statement represents a radical reversal of one's reality. We cannot earn more of God's love with accomplishments, success, or piety, or by doing any more of anything to please God. God loves each one of us fully and deeply as God's child. And likewise, as incomprehensible as this may be, there is nothing we can do to separate us from the love of God. Nothing. This is God's *good* news.

The first Christian act is therefore not a practice of obedience—of earning God's love. The first Christian act is to accept being loved by God, to experience the overwhelming giftedness and freedom that shapes a relationship with God in Jesus Christ, to understand oneself as "beloved." To understand the good news that God loves us so much is to reflect on the story of Advent and Christmas. God sent God's Son, Jesus Christ. Mary gave birth to Jesus, the Son of God, to live, teach, suffer, and die for our sins and the sins of the world. This is the miracle of Christmas and the meaning of Advent.

The season of Advent reminds Christians of the simple yet amazing salvation story, our story, the good news of God's love for all. We do not practice Advent for God, but rather for us. Advent is a gift. The season of Advent provides space to remember God's salvation for all creation in Christ. During Advent as a new Christian year begins, we prepare our hearts and spirits to embrace the wonder of God's love. Advent allows us, once again, to live into the freedom from sin and death through God's salvation. Reliving what God has done through the birth of Jesus Christ to Mary and Joseph, our hearts and minds are directed Godward. The following chapters offer a guide to reorient our focus from the distractions of this world to God's infinite love and goodness, preparing us for Jesus Christ's coming at Christmas.

"Good for All":
Receiving and Sharing God's Love

John Wesley, the founder of Methodism, in his "The Character of a Methodist," answered the questions "Who is a Methodist?" and "What is the mark?" with this response: "A Methodist is one who has the love of God shed abroad in [one's] heart" (CM, 9:35). For Wesley the marks of Methodism were not religious opinions or distinctive doctrinal commitments setting them apart from other Christians. Grounded in biblical texts, Wesley turned to the simple, and at the same time unimaginable, reality of God's love. This love embodied in Jesus Christ invites all to receive God's love and then to practice love through holiness of heart and life.

13

When our identities have been permeated by the "Beloved"-ness of knowing God's love for us and all creation, we are then empowered and animated to respond. We respond by fulfilling the great commandments to love God and neighbor by participating in good works. John Wesley and others in Christian tradition called these good works the "means of grace." The cultivation of practices of loving God and neighbor demonstrated by our participation in the means of grace in response to God's love for us frames the Christian faith.

The theme of love of God and neighbor is a persistent thread throughout the Bible. The refrain to care for widows, orphans, and strangers echoes throughout biblical texts as a response to God's love: from Israel's time as strangers in a strange land and later as a nation, through Jesus's birth and incarnation as God with us, as well as his ministry conveyed in the Gospels, into the early church described by the Epistles. This theme of loving God and neighbor is the heart of our Christian faith. Similar to the essentials of food, water, rest, relationships, and exercise to sustain human life, practices of loving God and neighbor provide the essentials for vital lives of faith within Christian community.

The symbol of the cross is a reminder of the two-dimensional character of our relationship with God. Through Jesus Christ's death on the cross and resurrection, God offers grace and love through reconciliation and forgiveness of our sins in the gift of salvation. The vertical portion of the cross represents God's gift of grace and love in Jesus Christ through the Holy Spirit. Our response to God's love and grace in Jesus Christ elicits our response of gratitude to God demonstrated in love and compassion to our neighbors. The horizontal portion of the cross demonstrates this love for and with our neighbors. In looking at the cross we remember God's love for all and our response in love to others and creation.

In this season of Advent, as we await the birth of the Christ child, may we remember and know God's goodness and love for us.

Overview of Chapters

In chapter 1, I begin by reflecting on Luke 3:4-6 and John the Baptist's call to "prepare the way of the Lord." This chapter addresses why Christians practice Advent. With other biblical texts, the chapter explores God's goodness and creation's need for God's grace in Jesus Christ. Good works do not earn God's grace; rather, they are our grateful response to God's love and a demonstration of our love for others. Drawing from John Wesley and the early Methodist movement, I describe God's grace as prevenient, justifying, and sanctifying. Good works—or means of grace, as Wesley called them—allow believers to respond to God's grace and participate in sharing God's love with others. Practices pursued by early Methodists, from keeping journals to providing microloans, offer examples for contemporary Christians to consider.

In chapter 2 Sangwoo Kim reflects on Luke 1 and Zechariah's prophecy of Jesus Christ's birth. Zechariah's devotion to God and openness to receive and share God's vision inspire our practices—especially practices of prayer during the season of Advent. Through prayer we listen for God's grace and guidance. As Wesley explains, prayer and works of piety cultivate an openness to receive God's love and vision for our lives. Praying in Advent prepares our hearts to receive Jesus Christ at Christmas and to follow God's call for sharing God's love with the world.

In chapter 3, Jung Choi reflects on Luke 1:46b-55 and the obedience of Mary and Joseph to follow God's call beyond their comfort and understanding. When we respond to God's call, even when unimaginable, the beauty of God's love for us, neighbors, and all creation unfolds. As Wesley demonstrates through his account of works of mercy, our response to God's love is always connected to love for all, including the poor and marginalized.

In chapter 4 Amy Valdez Barker reflects on Luke 2 and the birth of Christ from her own experience of being born on Christmas Eve and becoming a young mother similar to Mary. While Wesley maintains faith as central to salvation, Wesley encourages the early Methodists to allow God to perfect us in love. We receive perfection in love when we respond to God's grace by sharing God's love with others. Sharing God's love takes many forms, including service, advocacy, mission, education, and more. Through sharing God's love, God invites all to share in God's mission with Jesus Christ to the world.

We look forward to sharing this season of Advent in this collection of writings as we reflect on God's goodness in Jesus Christ through the Holy Spirit as we prepare for Christmas.

Chapter One

Practicing Advent

Preparing the Way

LACEYE WARNER

"Ready or Not, Here I Come!"

When I think of Advent and hear the biblical text describing John the Baptist, the excitement of playing the game of hide-and-seek comes to mind. One December, in the midst of a very patient and understanding congregation, I played hide-and-seek in the sanctuary with squealing and giggling children during an Advent worship service.

As I counted, some children hid under pews, another behind the pulpit, while others explored previously unnoticed corners of the narthex. After counting to twenty I announced, "Ready or not, here I come!" Some children peeked out to watch me search for them. Others held their breath in silent stillness. Several ran to the altar, our home base, while I continued my careful journey around the room.

Eventually, with each child found, we gathered, seated on the floor in front of the altar, to reflect on the Scripture text for that Sunday. In the text John the Baptist travels throughout the region, echoing the prophet Isaiah, "Prepare the way of the Lord." God called John to tell the people, "Ready or not, here I come!" What a wonderful way to prepare for Christmas.

Why Advent?

> *In the fifteenth year of the reign of Emperor Tiberius, when Pontius Pilate was governor of Judea, and Herod was ruler of Galilee, and his brother Philip ruler of the region of Ituraea and Trachonitis, and Lysanias ruler of Abilene, during the high priesthood of Annas and Caiaphas, the word of God came to John son of Zechariah in the wilderness. He went into all the region around the Jordan, proclaiming a baptism of repentance for the forgiveness of sins, as it is written in the book of the words of the prophet Isaiah,*
>
> > *"The voice of one crying out in the wilderness:*
> > *'Prepare the way of the Lord,*
> >   *make his paths straight.*

Every valley shall be filled,
and every mountain and hill shall be
made low,
and the crooked shall be made straight,
and the rough ways made smooth;
and all flesh shall see the salvation of God.'"

John said to the crowds that came out to be baptized
by him, "You brood of vipers! Who warned you to flee
from the wrath to come?"

Luke 3:1-7

Advent begins with the acknowledgment of our need and desire for God. In this text, God calls John the Baptist to announce the approaching arrival of Jesus Christ. John described God's desire for relationship and called for people to be baptized in response to God's love and forgiveness. In other gospel texts, John explains humanity's need for God to heal the separation that occurred when sin entered the world as a result of Adam and Eve's fall. The season of Advent marks a time and space to prepare to receive God's presence in the birth of Jesus Christ that overcomes the separation that sin continues to inflict on our world.

In the beginning, as Genesis narrates, God created the earth and all its creatures, including Adam and Eve. After eating the forbidden fruit Adam and Eve realize they are naked. When they hear the sound of God walking in the garden, Adam and Eve hide themselves from God among the trees. God calls to them, "Where are you?" Adam responds, "I heard the sound of you in the garden, and I was afraid, because I was naked; and I hid myself." God said, "Who told you that you were naked?" In Genesis, the story of sin entering the world continues. Christian tradition refers to this tragic event in salvation history as the Fall (Genesis 3).

Throughout biblical texts the same story unfolds repeatedly in different scenes with a range of characters from Noah to King David to Paul. God creates goodness. Humanity sins. God invites relationship, offering forgiveness and salvation. Advent represents the climax of this story line. God sends the ultimate invitation in Jesus Christ, fully human and fully divine, born into the world to inaugurate God's reign and redeem all of creation from the power of sin and death.

Without a diagnosis of an illness, a cure is not possible. At times sin invades as a chronic condition, steadily disintegrating and distorting our understanding of the world. At other times, sin destroys violently, whether individually or corporately, through systems of evil. Relationship with God cures the world's disease of sin and death.

During Advent we participate in the salvation story, which culminates in God's sending Jesus Christ to embody God's love for all creation. The salvation story invites our response to God's good gift in Jesus Christ through the Holy Spirit. Christians respond to God's love with love for God and others. We express this love, according to John Wesley, by cultivating "fruits meet for repentance" (SSWS, 3:2) through good works, also called means of grace. In Advent, and particularly the first week of Advent, we reflect on God's love and grace in Jesus Christ and begin or begin again practices of receiving and sharing God's grace.

All the Good: God's Grace

To prepare for practicing God's means of grace in Advent, let us reflect on what Christianity understands about God's grace, learning specifically from Augustine and John Wesley. God's grace encompasses God's love and forgiveness in Jesus Christ through the Holy Spirit for all. Grace can be misunderstood as a spiritual credit card or bank account balance. For example, one misconception claims God grants a finite amount of grace to each person at baptism, and we then spend that grace on minor or major infractions, occasionally adding to our balance with good works. This concept of grace is wrong. Grace is not finite; it is infinite. Rather than something God dispenses as a commodity, grace is relationship with God. It is an infinite abundance of love and goodness God offers us in relationship with God and all creation.

God's Goodness and Grace: Augustine on Psalm 51

First, let us reflect on how Christians can misunderstand God's grace, which is such an important aspect of Advent and Christmas. In the following section Augustine helps us recognize ways we focus too narrowly on ourselves rather than on the vastness of God's grace and love. Acknowledged by church tradition as one of the seven penitential psalms, Psalm 51 highlights themes of confession and God's grace. Although most likely written much later, the text sets its petitions against the background of King David's transgressions. For generations, this psalm has been prayed by Christians on Ash Wednesday during the season of Lent. While Ash Wednesday, Lent, and Easter may seem very distant from Advent, these seasons are closely related—for there is no Lent or Easter without Advent and Christmas.

> *Have mercy on me, O God,*
> *according to your steadfast love;*
> *according to your abundant mercy*
> *blot out my transgressions.*
> *Wash me thoroughly from my iniquity,*
> *and cleanse me from my sin.*
>
> *For I know my transgressions,*
> *and my sin is ever before me.*
> *Against you, you alone, have I sinned,*
> *and done what is evil in your sight,*
> *so that you are justified in your sentence*
> *and blameless when you pass judgment.*
> *Indeed, I was born guilty,*
> *a sinner when my mother conceived me.*
>
> *You desire truth in the inward being;*
> *therefore teach me wisdom in my secret heart.*
> *Purge me with hyssop, and I shall be clean;*
> *wash me, and I shall be whiter than snow.*
> *Let me hear joy and gladness;*
> *let the bones that you have crushed rejoice.*
> *Hide your face from my sins,*
> *and blot out all my iniquities.*

Create in me a clean heart, O God,
and put a new and right spirit within me.
Do not cast me away from your presence,
and do not take your holy spirit from me.
Restore to me the joy of your salvation,
and sustain in me a willing spirit.

Then I will teach transgressors your ways,
and sinners will return to you.

Psalm 51:1-13

Augustine, in his commentary on Psalm 51 in *Exposition on the Psalms*, identifies the tendency of focusing too narrowly on *me* and *my sin* during confession, and not focusing enough on God and God's grace. Although contemplation of one's individual sinfulness is an important practice, by starting and ending with one's individual sinfulness, one misses the larger landscape against which the psalm is set. Similarly, when focusing on Advent or Lent, an individual may miss the larger landscape of Christmas and Easter upon which the salvation story is set.

To pray Psalm 51 reciting the familiar themes of sin and confession, identifying with the psalmist's, possibly King David's, transgressions can result in missing the abundant landscape of God's grace, steadfast love, and compassion that illumines the background. In Psalm 51, God's character is the focus, specifically God's gracious goodness. The psalmist is not searching for God or strategizing to change God. Rather, the psalmist possesses an intimate knowledge of God. There is a closeness in the relationship presumed. The petitions are not prayed to a distant or remote God, but to a God who is known intimately and intimately knows the one who prays. In this knowledge of God, the psalmist gains a clear view of and perspective on sins.

In *Exposition on the Psalms*, Augustine is concerned that we do not perceive our sins appropriately. For example, David, a great man, sinned excessively—adultery and murder. Therefore, most of us breathe a sigh of relief, since David has established a substantially steep curve for sinning. Because David sinned so excessively—and God forgave him so graciously—we can be assured of God's grace.

Not only, according to Augustine, are we assured of God's grace, since most likely we are not nearly as sinful as David, but we perceive David's fallenness as permissive. By looking to David's transgressions, some actually incline themselves to sin, not to penitence or holiness. In this self-centered theme, David's transgressions become an example implicitly to permit lesser sins. This view focuses wrongly on our lesser sinfulness in comparison to David's, rather than the graciousness of God, missing the glorious landscape of a life of holiness in relationship with God through Jesus Christ in the Holy Spirit.

This dynamic of implicit permission for sinning at times characterizes our life together. Instead of focusing on God's grace for all creation, we focus on contrasting ourselves with one another, highlighting degrees of sinfulness. Or we engage in a related but equally destructive tendency: we compete with one another for worldly favor, measuring accomplishments. The disease of sins pervasive in our world pales in comparison to the abundant grace and joy found in relationship to God and neighbors. It is so very difficult for humans to imagine the infinite, and especially to imagine the infinite abundance of God's love and grace for each one of us and all creation.

John Wesley and Grace

Grace echoes throughout the biblical narratives of Advent and Christmas. And grace underscores John Wesley's entire theology and practice of ministry. Grace, for John Wesley, is God's presence and power to save and transform individuals, societies, and the whole of creation. In one of his most often preached sermons and the most comprehensive example of his mature theological reflection, *The Scripture Way of Salvation* (1765), Wesley describes his understanding of grace (SWS, 2:153–69). Drawing on biblical texts and themes as well as Christian tradition, John Wesley describes grace in three roles: *preventing* (prevenient), *justifying*, and *sanctifying*.

Prevenient grace goes before, preceding human effort or response. It is universally present, prompting, convicting, wooing, and preparing us to accept God's invitation into relationship. Grace always precedes human awareness, effort, and response. Prevenient grace meets us in creation, neighbors, and strangers. It also surpasses our human chronological understanding of God's unfolding salvation story. This means that God's sending Jesus Christ with the Holy Spirit to the world redeems all throughout history, since God is not bound by time and space. Through prevenient grace, God's grace extends to all in time and space, including, for example, Abraham and Sarah, among many others in and beyond the people of Israel. God's salvation story enters our imagination through prevenient grace.

Universal atonement offers a bridge between prevenient and justifying grace by emphasizing the offer of God's grace to all—universally. This does not mean all accept that grace, since God included free choice as an aspect of creation—hence, the fall of Adam and Eve. Universal atonement describes God's grace, which is available to all of God's creation. At times this understanding of God's grace causes controversy. Universal atonement can be confused with a misconception of salvation that depends on human actions and choice. For John Wesley, as well as Christian tradition, salvation is never dependent upon human choice or works. Only God saves, and God saves through grace alone and not by any human effort.

Justifying grace is God's presence to forgive, save, and reconcile us to God and one another. It confirms our identity as beloved and forgiven children of God with divinely bestowed worth and dignity. Through justifying grace, we receive assurance that our sins are forgiven. God claims us as beloved sons and daughters. God acts decisively in Jesus Christ to restore the divine image in us. Justifying grace is what God does for us through Jesus Christ.

Sanctifying grace is God's presence and power, through the Holy Spirit, to form and shape us in the image of Christ, perfect us in love, and create in us "holiness of heart and life" (SSWS, 3.15).

Sanctifying grace enables us to "go on to perfection" (SSWS, 1:9). It is a process of growth as we respond through practicing the means of grace—works of piety and works of mercy. Good works are not possible before receiving justifying grace because these would be works seeking righteous, which is God's alone to give. Sanctifying grace is what God does in us through the Holy Spirit, cultivating a heart and life of holiness within and through us.

Though Wesley argued faith in response to grace as the only requirement for salvation, with biblical texts, Wesley considered good works to be significant aspects of one's faith. "God does undoubtedly command us both to repent and to bring forth fruits meet for repentance....But they are not necessary in the *same sense* with faith, nor in the *same degree*...for those fruits are only necessary *conditionally*, if there be time and opportunity for them" (SSWS, 2:162–63). Wesley emphasized that Christian practices are merely *means* of receiving God's grace and not *ends*, thus avoiding the danger of works righteousness.

For Wesley, such practices were pursued in response to God's justifying gift of grace in Jesus Christ as a component of sanctification. Wesley encouraged believers to pursue works of piety and mercy. According to Wesley, "God is both able and willing to sanctify us *now*" (SSWS, 2:168). However, Wesley explained that works of piety and mercy are "the fruits meet for repentance...necessary to full sanctification. This is the way wherein God hath appointed his children to wait for complete salvation" (SSWS, 2:166). According to John Wesley's sermon *Scripture Way of Salvation,* works of piety and works of mercy are necessary to a Christian's sanctification. However, these fruits are not necessary in the same sense or to the same degree as faith. According to Wesley, a person may be sanctified without them, but may not be sanctified without faith, and then if there be time and opportunity, the fruits become necessary.

"Watching over One Another in Love": Early Methodists

John Wesley described means of grace as "the ordinary channels of conveying [God's] grace into the souls of [human beings]." Practicing the means of grace was a way of cultivating lives of holiness, remembering and participating in God's love and grace. However, practicing spiritual disciplines can be extremely difficult—even during Advent and Christmas. Wesley felt that the means of grace should be used constantly, combining the inner with the outer expressions of salvation. Drawing from John Wesley and the early Methodist movement, the following section describes the means of grace and helpful aspects for their practice—small groups, accountability, and specific practices of piety and mercy. Practicing the means of grace, loving God and neighbor, is a wonderful way to respond to God's love, especially during Advent, as we prepare for Christmas.

Small Groups

John, with his brother Charles, oversaw the organization of the early Methodist movement with intentional connectedness.

The Methodist renewal movement facilitated mutual support and accountability and fulfilled the movement's aim to form believers in holiness of heart and life. The distinctiveness of the early Methodist movement was not in its novelty or innovation, but in its simple, yet profound, integration of doctrine and discipline toward an authentic Christianity through an intentionally comprehensive program of preaching and small groups.

The vitality of the early Methodist renewal movement depended on small group gatherings. John consistently urged that authentic spiritual formation could not take place "without society, without living and conversing with [others]" (SSM, 1:533–34). In Wesley's account of the Methodist renewal movement, *A Plain Account of the People Called Methodists*, most of the pamphlet addresses organization and practices of the movement, particularly small group gatherings. In response to pleas for spiritual nurture, John and Charles Wesley facilitated regular small group gatherings. These gatherings resembled religious societies common among the Church of England and European Pietists.

Gatherings grew into networks of Methodist circuits across Britain. Classes consisted of ten to twelve participants and were organized geographically, meaning those who lived in close proximity to one another gathered. All participants in the Methodist movement gathered in a class meeting. Some participants also gathered in a band. Band meetings were smaller, numbering approximately six to eight, and were organized around a common experience. Today, bands might be called affinity groups, organized according to age, gender, and/or marital status. The movement's gatherings, specifically classes and bands, provided opportunities for early Methodist laypersons, including women and young adults, to assume leadership roles (PPCM, 9:254–80).

General Rules: Covenant through Accountability

To encourage nurture and accountability, small group participants adhered to three guiding principles. John Wesley called these the General Rules. Though simple in nature, these rules remain a part of United Methodism's formal doctrinal materials along with the Articles of Religion, EUB Confession of Faith, and Wesley's *Sermons and Notes on the New Testament*. The General Rules for the United Societies describe the small group gatherings as "a company of [persons] having the form and seeking the power of godliness, united in order to pray together, receive words of exhortation, and to watch over one another in love, that they may help each other to work out their salvation."[1]

The one condition for admission to a small group remained "a desire to flee from the wrath to come, to be saved from their sins" (PPCM, 9:257). Continuing attendance in small groups required practicing the general rules. The early Methodists practiced the following three general rules: (1) do no harm, and avoid evil of every kind; (2) do good; and (3) attend upon the ordinances of God—including the means of grace or works of piety and mercy. The General Rules facilitated mutual support and provided a guide for accountability.

Impact of Small Groups: An Experiment

Although George Whitefield's and the Wesleys' preaching, particularly in the open air, is well documented for its impact on British as well as North American Christianity, their preaching did not stand alone as an effective strategy for outreach. Significant to understanding preaching as one aspect of the early Methodist renewal movement is its practice alongside small groups.

In 1745 the Methodist Conference under John's leadership decided to experiment with preaching wherever opportunities arose, first in Wales and Cornwall, then later in the north, without forming societies, or regardless of the presence of societies, to nurture those responding. The results of the experiment were unequivocal. Christian formation provided by the Methodist small groups organized by John Wesley allowed a significant number of those moved by the revival's preaching to be nurtured and maintained in the faith. When these groups were not accessible, those moved by the preaching were often lost. The experiment ceased in 1748, and the conference turned its focus to the formation of societies.

While John, Charles, and Whitefield attracted substantial crowds with their field preaching, these venues were less frequently occasions for spiritual experiences. Key spiritual experiences, such as conviction or awakening, new birth, and sanctification, occurred more frequently in small groups than in preaching events. In a study conducted by Rev. Dr. Tom Albin, former dean of the Upper Room, Albin discovered that more than half of early Methodists received a spiritual experience within the first year of participation in a small group. According to Albin's study, laypeople were more influential than clergy in facilitating key spiritual experiences. Early Methodist conversions occurred most often in solitude, followed by small groups.[2]

Means of Grace

Wesley divided the means of grace into two groups: works of piety and works of mercy (or charity). Wesley called works of piety "instituted means of grace" because according to the Gospels, Jesus Christ instituted these practices. Wesley called works of mercy "prudential means of grace" because practicing these is prudent—and consistent with Christian practices.

> "But what good works are those, the practice of which you affirm to be necessary to sanctification?"
>
> First, all works of piety, such as public prayer, family prayer, and praying in our closet; receiving the Supper of the Lord; searching the Scriptures by hearing, reading, meditating, and using such a measure of fasting or abstinence as our bodily health allows.
>
> Secondly, all works of mercy, whether they relate to the bodies or souls of men; such as feeding the hungry, clothing the naked, entertaining the stranger, visiting those that are in prison, or sick, or variously afflicted; such as the endeavouring

> to instruct the ignorant, to awaken the sinner, to
> quicken the lukewarm, to confirm the wavering, to
> comfort the feebleminded, to succour the tempted,
> or contribute in any manner to the saving of souls
> from death. (SSWS, 2:166)

Participants in small groups encouraged one another in their Christian journeys through works of piety, such as public and private prayer, study of scripture, confession, and fasting, as well as praise and worship. These practices were means of grace through which individuals might come to faith in Jesus Christ and have that faith nurtured and deepened through spiritual growth.

In addition to works of piety, small group participants also engaged in works of mercy, addressing the bodies as well as souls of individuals. Works of mercy included feeding the hungry, clothing the naked, and visiting the imprisoned, sick, and afflicted. John prioritized works of mercy over works of piety because of the perception that works of mercy are more difficult to practice.

From the time of John and Charles Wesley's participation in the Holy Club at Oxford during the earliest years of the Wesleyan movement, works of mercy represented a significant commitment of time and spiritual discipline. An early influence on John Wesley and early Methodists to participate in works of mercy, William Morgan, led the group to regularly visit prisons, teach orphaned children, and care for the poor and aged. John Wesley encouraged the people called Methodists throughout his lifetime to participate in works of piety and mercy, since such activities demonstrated evidence of the presence of sanctifying grace cultivating lives of holiness going on to Christian perfection.

To address systems of oppressive poverty, Wesley organized educational opportunities, medical dispensaries, and microlending resources. Beginning in 1739, Wesley carried out the plan Whitefield had initially conceived of building a school for the coal-mining families of Kingswood, holding together knowledge and vital piety in the early Methodist renewal movement. The conference deliberated on the details of the rules, as well as the curriculum, which instructed children on topics from the alphabet to preparation for ministry. Subjects included reading, writing, arithmetic, French, Latin, Greek, Hebrew, rhetoric, geography, chronology, history, logic, ethics, physics, geometry, algebra, and music. Wesley wrote grammars for the English and other language courses and claimed that upon completing the Kingswood curriculum, a student would be a better scholar than 90 percent of those completing degrees at Oxford and Cambridge.

Alongside his contributions to the Kingswood School's curriculum, Wesley also compiled the Christian Library for the education of Methodists and its preachers. Begun in 1749, the extensive publishing project was completed in 1755, largely at Wesley's own expense. The Christian Library made accessible significant pieces of practical divinity published in English. Consisting of fifty volumes arranged chronologically from the early church, the project was meant to give readers access to the most eminent authors and works of Christian tradition.

John Wesley facilitated several experiments in outreach from the Foundery in London, including a lending stock and a medical dispensary. These demonstrated Wesley's pastoral wisdom to treat both symptoms and systems of poverty, empowering many Methodists not merely to survive, but to live sustainably and even flourish. In the early decades of the Methodist renewal movement, many of those attracted to the classes and band meetings, mostly women and youth/young adults, were impoverished. In the later decades of the eighteenth century, following the movement's consolidation, those active in the movement represented in greater numbers the middle classes, possibly demonstrating a long-term effectiveness of such programs and the support of new institutional contexts.

Wesley had hoped that the Methodist movement would eventually have all things in common. This proved difficult to coordinate and was increasingly complicated as the movement grew. In 1746, Wesley experimented with a different economic assistance program: the lending stock, a sort of microloan program funded by a collection among Wesley's more affluent friends in London. Two stewards were appointed from the society to hold the fifty pounds collected for disbursement in zero- or low-interest loans up to twenty shillings (one British pound) at the Foundery each Tuesday morning. The microloans could be used for financial relief, but they could also be used to assist small business owners/managers. The loans were disbursed to members of Methodist societies, who had to pledge their repayment within three months. In the first year, the lending stock assisted 250 people.

John Wesley pursued a lifelong interest in medicine, demonstrated in part by his publication *Primitive Physick: Or, An Easy and Natural Method of Curing Most Diseases.* He published the text anonymously in 1747, eventually putting his name to it as author in 1760. Skeptical of the effectiveness of physicians, and most likely moved by those too poor to gain access to medical care, he began stocking a number of the preaching houses with medicines. After consulting with those trained in the medical field, he engaged a surgeon and an apothecary to help him in late 1746 to implement a regular system of dispensing medicine at the Foundery each Friday. Thus, in December 1746, the Foundery became a medical dispensary in accord with Wesley's intention of "giving physic to the poor" and treating those with chronic rather than acute illnesses. Following Wesley's announcement, the Foundery's medical dispensary soon grew to a steady monthly clientele of approximately one hundred visitors at an annual cost of less than 120 pounds. When treatments were effective in relieving some ailments, Wesley was quick to refer to God's work in all things. Unlike the lending stock, medical dispensary services were not limited to members of the Foundery Society. Similar medical dispensaries were also generally present at the preaching houses in Bristol and Newcastle.

Practicing Advent

The season of Advent allows space and time to reflect on God's grace in Jesus Christ offered to the world. Advent, particularly the first week in Advent, invites Christians to reflect on and respond to God's grace through beginning, or beginning again, practices of the means of grace—for personal spiritual growth and to shape corporate responses to systemic sin. Modern themes of self-sufficiency and desire for immediate results often result in apathy for sustained Christian practices. Christian practices, particularly means of grace, offer Christians a pattern of spiritual formation to follow.

Christian practices of piety and mercy can consist of simple daily practices—and can be a helpful way to reflect on the meaning of Advent in preparation for Christmas. The goal is not to accomplish a task through the practice, but rather to open a space—a means—to receive God's grace and formation in God's image. While it is commendable to read the entire Bible in a month or a year, the practice loses its meaning if the reader does not gain a deeper relationship with God and the world through the practice of reading. Through simple regular spiritual practices during Advent, we can build habits that nurture our relationship with God and others all year long.

Practicing the means of grace is similar to tending a garden. The gardener prepares the soil, distributes water, plants seeds, and daily supports the seeds through germination, growth, and fruit. However, the gardener does not have the power to create the seed, sunlight, or water, or to cause it to grow and produce fruit. The gardener *participates* in the cultivation of the growth and fruit. However, the miracle of the seed, its growth, and its fruit come from *God*. In this way gardening is similar to practicing the means of grace. When we read biblical texts, pray in silence, worship, and serve together, we participate in God's reign while God pours out divine grace and love into our lives and the world.

Practicing means of grace requires balance and discipline. For example, a garden that produces fruit needs a different discipline and balance than a swamp. Both a garden and a swamp contain an abundance of life. However, the garden produces fruit that nourishes and sustains creation. Life in a swamp, though it possesses a distinct kind of beauty, does not nourish or sustain in the same ways as a garden. Swamps consist of excess, even flooding, rather than a disciplined balance. A garden requires balance and discipline in participation with God to produce fruit. During Advent we have the opportunity to practice this balance and discipline in preparation for Christ's coming at Christmas. The following are examples drawn from Wesley of participating in practices that remind us of God's grace for us and encourage us to share God's grace with others.

Care of Time

We have already noted that John Wesley's definition of means of grace is "the ordinary channels of conveying [God's] grace into the souls of [human beings]." As noted earlier, he felt that means of grace should be used constantly, combining the inner with the outer expressions of God's grace. An important component of early Methodist practices of means of grace, alongside small groups and their accountability, was the care of one's time through keeping a diary. Let's apply this to our gardening illustration. A garden thrives when there is even a small amount of daily attention, but rapidly declines with long periods of neglect, requiring great effort to get things back on track. Similarly, the use of our time each day supports our cultivation of faith and trust in God—in both ourselves and in others.

John Wesley learned early in his spiritual journey the importance of one's use of time as a daily discipline. He was strongly influenced by Jeremy Taylor's book *Holy Living and Holy Dying* (1650). Wesley's response was to keep a diary. Wesley used his diary to document the use of his time, which he reflected on with others to inform his own spiritual formation and specifically discern needs related to his sanctification toward holy living. Wesley discovered that holiness was an inner reality—"that true religion was seated in the heart and that God's law extended to all our thoughts as well as words and actions" (JD, 18:244).

John and Charles Wesley, with other classmates and colleagues at Oxford participating in the Holy Club, each committed to keep a diary of their participation in the means of grace. An aspect of keeping diaries in addition to recording activities was evaluating one's "temper" during the activity on a numerical scale of 1 to 9. John Wesley usually recorded his daily activities in hourly intervals, but occasionally recorded them in fifteen-minute intervals. He also regularly posed as many as twenty questions to guide the evaluation of his daily activities. For example:

Have I prayed with fervor regularly throughout the day?

Have I after every pleasure immediately given thanks?

Did I in the morning plan the business of the day?

Has good will been and appeared the spring of all my actions toward others?

Have I been or seemed angry?

Have I thought or spoken unkindly of or to anyone?

Have I felt or entertained or seemed to approve any proud, vain, or unchaste thought?

Have I been particularly recollect, temperate, and thankful in eating or drinking?

(JD, 1730)

To avoid unwelcome derision, the Holy Club participants developed a cipher or code in which to record activities in their diaries. When small groups met, participants would share their diaries with one another, inviting encouragement, constructive criticism, and guidance.

A possible Advent practice and participation in the means of grace is keeping a journal throughout Advent to help us reflect on our use of time. Reflecting on our use of time helps us to notice how God's grace shapes our identity, action, and purpose.

Practicing God's Love in Community

A tiny British Methodist church was facing a looming challenge. They had dwindled over the years until there were just eight people—and that was on the Sundays when everyone could attend. They had done all they knew to do to "reach out to young people" and grow the church, but to no avail.

A time finally came when the matriarch and heart of the church reached an age and situation when she could no longer live alone. She moved into a nursing home not too far away from the church. The congregation was heartbroken that their beloved friend and mentor would no longer be able to worship with them. Since they were a dying church anyway, why not have a grand gesture to still include their friend? They decided to move their worship every fourth Sunday to the nursing home, so they could all worship together.

The first Sunday in the nursing home, seventy people participated in the worship service; the second Sunday almost double that number participated. It was not long before the church decided to meet regularly at the nursing home, finding growth through reaching out to the aging, who longed for a place to worship, and not the young, whom the church previously assumed they needed to survive. They reached out in selfless ministry, participating in means of grace, the kind that only imminent closure freed them to consider, and there they met Jesus and the unusual unfolding of the reign of God. Even in the midst of grief and change, like that experienced by this congregation, God's grace persists. By participating in means of grace, individuals and communities open a space to receive God's grace and share God's grace with others.

Building on the Advent practice of journaling mentioned in the last section, another Advent practice is to discern in a small group or congregation which means of grace will be practiced in preparation for Christmas. Naming the means of grace that individuals will practice, as well as practices to pursue as a group or congregation, demonstrates care concerning the use of our shared time and shapes our witness as the body of Christ in the world.

Persistent Practices: Mary McLeod Bethune

Mary McLeod Bethune (1875–1955) made astonishing achievements in her lifetime. She was the first African American woman to establish a four-year institution of higher learning and to found a national organization to lobby the federal government, and the first African American of either gender to hold such a high-level government appointment as director of the Negro Division of the National Youth Administration. She advised three presidents and received numerous awards. Between 1933 and 1945, Bethune was arguably the most powerful African American *individual* in the United States. According to her, this was largely due to the exercise of her Christian faith, including simple daily practices of means of grace, such as devotion and works of piety, out of which her accomplishments grew. Bethune described her formation as being raised in a loving Christian home and in local church communities in which she learned disciplined Christian practices that provided the foundation for her life and vocation.

In reflecting on her life in her essay "Spiritual Autobiography," Bethune explained the significance of "meditation and communion" alone with God for her continued spiritual growth after the example of her mother. "I feel [God] working in and through me, and I have learned to give myself—freely—unreservedly to the guidance of the inner voice in me."[3] Bethune acknowledged that she gained faith from watching her mother pursue Christian practices, such as reading the Bible and prayer, and from witnessing those prayers answered. These practices, shaped by regular reading of the biblical texts and prayer, were not isolated from material needs, but rather demonstrated the necessary connection between practices of love of God and neighbor.

God's Presence

Advent provides space to prepare for God's arrival in the birth of Jesus Christ to Mary and Joseph in a Bethlehem manger. It is a time when Christians seek God, Emmanuel—God with us—in Jesus of Nazareth. Advent also indicates a season for preparation and searching as we pursue Christian practices as means of God's grace. However, what we find when immersed in means of grace is that we do not need to find God, for God in Jesus Christ, through the Holy Spirit, has found us—and indeed God has been present all along. Practicing means of grace, practicing Advent, reminds us that God loves us so abundantly. There is no longer any need to hide.

Mary McLeod Bethune's words describe our Advent call:

> The church is beginning to acquire new courage in the application to life of the great moral truths.... But too often these principles are merely preached in beautiful language when there is the pressing need to set them forth in the specific language of deed.[4]

Prayer

Lord, make me an instrument of Your peace. Where there is hatred, let me sow love; where there is injury, pardon; where there is doubt, faith; where there is despair, hope; where there is darkness, light; where there is sadness, joy.

O, Divine Master, grant that I may not so much seek to be consoled as to console; to be understood as to understand; to be loved as to love; For it is in giving that we receive; it is in pardoning that we are pardoned; it is in dying that we are born again to eternal life.

Saint Francis

Chapter Two
Praying in Advent

SANGWOO KIM

Both Lent and Advent are liturgical seasons of intensive preparation for the good news. We eagerly but patiently wait for the news of Christ's resurrection (in Lent) and incarnation (in Advent). The liturgical color of both seasons is purple, which signifies repentance and royalty. It is an interesting juxtaposition of two seemingly contrasting themes. On the one hand, we intently reflect on our sinful brokenness: broken selves, broken relationships, broken promises of justice, and broken dreams of beauty and harmony. On the other hand, we focus on who Christ our King is and what he can do in us, with us, and for us. Without repentance, without recognizing what we fail to be and do, we would not truly see our need for Christ. Without our hope in Christ the King and the new creation in him, our repentance would produce despair; the more we honestly look at our problems, the more we realize the solution is not within us. Lent and Advent help to keep us focused on both problem and hope.

In both Lent and Advent, we simultaneously look backward and forward. We look back at the past events: Christ's resurrection and incarnation. We look forward to the fulfillment of God's promises: Christ's second coming and our resurrection. I love the seasons of Advent and Christmas. The thoughts of Christmas lights and decorations, festivity, family time, and sacred music warm my heart. But more important, in the rhythm of remembrance and anticipation, Advent guides me to go deeper in my practices of discernment and imagination, and prayer plays a central role in this time of reflection and preparation.

Needless to say, prayer is an essential practice of Christian life. It is so essential that I think it is unthinkable for us to be Christians without praying. It does not mean that prayer is a merit necessary for us to be qualified as Christians. I mean it is difficult to imagine one can sustain a Christian life without prayer. Despite its importance, however, many faithful people still struggle to pray consistently, not to mention without ceasing (see 1 Thessalonians 5:17). One would imagine the church would put a great effort into teaching and supporting us to pray well. But most people I meet in my ministry tell me that they never learned how to pray. "Just follow your heart," they were simply told. The strength of this advice would be authenticity found in spontaneity, the holy grail of prayer after Romanticism. But it overlooks the reality that our hearts are not often in a good place. Too often, they are distracted, perplexed, or uninterested. This strategy might work if prayer were merely a momentary expression of our feelings.

If we are interested in sustaining a prayerful life, we need more structured support and practice. A liturgical season is one of many such patterns of life in which we get habituated in Christ's story. Every year, we tell the entire story of Jesus through the church calendar: his birth, baptism, ministry, teaching, transfiguration, suffering, death, resurrection, ascension, sending of the Holy Spirit, and promised second coming. By doing so, we locate our stories in Christ's, and over time our prayer life gets shaped and reshaped in the liturgical cycle. In this Advent, I invite you to reflect on how the story of Christ's incarnation can enrich our understanding of prayer and Christian life.

Understanding a Life of Prayer

Sustaining a healthy prayer life is difficult, but it is not because we lack interest or desire to pray well. It is easy to shame people because nobody can live up to the standard of praying without ceasing. But I believe most of us have a genuine desire to pray. We have trouble praying consistently because we all experience some dreadful moments: when it feels like talking to a wall, when our words sound so trivial compared to a heavy weight we carry, when our desperate requests are not granted, or when we are afraid of what God might tell us to do. Sometimes we lament that God is not speaking to us, but sometimes we fear that God might speak to us. We would rather not know than deal with difficult messages. We would rather avoid talking to God because we know deep down in our hearts that God will tell us to forgive and love our enemies.

Prayer also makes us feel vulnerable. In our prayers of praise, confession, thanksgiving, and petition, we discover who God is and who we truly are. I often say our prayers can reveal our understanding of God, self, and world more than our theological statements do. Standing before God in prayer, we see how pointless our pretense is; we learn we cannot hide behind our lofty words because the Holy Spirit penetrates deep into our hearts. We might even feel naked in the presence of God. Prayer reveals multiple layers of our hearts, and we confront our greed, violence, hatred, and prejudice as well as our joy, faith, hope, and love. Our honest conversations with God can uncover the ocean of our desires, and it can be an overwhelming and even disorienting experience. Therefore, prayer is more than an act of delivering a list of requests. It draws us into an intimate relationship with God, in which we get to know God and ourselves more deeply. Such intimacy with God and with our own selves can be both exciting and frightening.

The more we pray, the more we realize how unruly our hearts are and the limitations of our knowledge. That humble experience makes us wonder what the point of our petitionary prayers is. Our desires might run amok, and our vision is imperfect, but

God already knows our needs better than we do. Then why do we still need to bring our petitions to God? The simple answer might be "Because God said so." But I think there is a deeper answer here. Despite our frustration, we can still boldly offer our petitions because Christ is our mediator, representing the whole of humanity, raising us up as his siblings. Christ, fully human and fully divine, stands beside all God's children and intercedes for us.

Those who pray are incorporated into Christ, who is in unity with God the Father. We never come to God as an absolute other; instead, we find ourselves in the mysterious work of the Trinity, who is both the speaker and listener of prayer. In our voices, God the Father hears the voice of the interceding Christ. Our prayer is not our own accomplishment but rather God's gift of grace coming through the Holy Spirit, who frees, enables, and incites us to pray. When we cannot find words for prayer, the Holy Spirit also "intercedes with sighs too deep" for human language (Romans 8:26). So, in our prayer, we not only speak but also almost overhear what the three persons of the Trinity exchange in words and sighs, and we join the circular movement of love that comes from God and returns to God. So, in our prayer, we can find the utmost hope and trust in the triune God.

It does not mean that our prayer is a simple dictation of the divine will. Jesus's own struggle, encapsulated in his prayer in the garden of Gethsemane (Matthew 26:36-46), brings the whole of humanity's struggle into the trinitarian relationship. In prayers of petition, lamentation, and thanksgiving, our desires undergo radical transformation. This process of transformation can be agonizing. Even Jesus's surrendering to God the Father ("yet not what I want but what you want" and "your will be done," Matthew 6:10; 26:39) was not passive resignation. In Gethsemane, both God the Son on the earth and God the Father in heaven experienced the crisis of humanity. Jesus's prayerful struggle was the epitome of humanity's struggle in prayer.

Anyone who takes prayer seriously has an experience of praying for a dying child, justice for the innocent, or the end of a horrible war, or getting deeply hurt. So, we stop talking to God, almost like giving God the silent treatment. Our struggle is not necessarily a sign of unbelief; it is a painful recognition of the reality that God's promise has not been fully fulfilled on earth yet. Thus, in Jesus's own wailing prayer, our broken hearts find that Christ already walked on the agonizing path before us and walks again with and for us now. In that discovery, we also find that the greatest answer to all prayers is Christ himself. Christ has come to us!

Becoming Christian: Made, Not Born

"Blessed be the Lord God of Israel,
for he has looked favorably on his people and
redeemed them.
He has raised up a mighty savior for us
in the house of his servant David,
as he spoke through the mouth of his holy prophets
from of old,
that we would be saved from our enemies and
from the hand of all who hate us.

Thus he has shown the mercy promised to our
ancestors,
    and has remembered his holy covenant,
the oath that he swore to our ancestor Abraham,
    to grant us that we, being rescued from the
    hands of our enemies,
might serve him without fear, in holiness and
righteousness
    before him all our days.
And you, child, will be called the prophet of the
Most High;
    for you will go before the Lord to prepare
    his ways,
to give knowledge of salvation to his people
    by the forgiveness of their sins.
By the tender mercy of our God,
    the dawn from on high will break upon us,
to give light to those who sit in darkness and in the
shadow of death,
    to guide our feet into the way of peace."

                                 Luke 1:68-79

Luke's Gospel begins with a story of an old childless couple "living blamelessly" (1:6): Zechariah and Elizabeth. Zechariah was a priest. When he was offering incense in the sanctuary, an angel appeared to him and said that the couple would have a son, and they should name him John. The child would be "great in the sight of the Lord" and "filled with the Holy Spirit" and would turn many people of Israel to God (1:15-16). Zechariah could not believe it. The angel said that because of his unbelief, Zechariah would not be able to speak again until this prophecy was fulfilled.

Indeed, Elizabeth became pregnant, and during her pregnancy, she spent three months with Mary, who was also miraculously pregnant with the Son of God. I always wonder how these two great mothers spent their time together. What did they talk, pray, and dream about? How did they proclaim the mysterious works of the Holy Spirit to each other? How did Elizabeth mentor Mary in this challenging time of transition and preparation? How did their solidarity shape their parenting? I often imagine myself sitting next to them, watching them sharing joy, fear, faith, hope, and all other kinds of emotions new parents typically experience.

After Elizabeth gave birth to a son, people wanted to name him Zechariah, after his father. But to their surprise, Elizabeth said his name should be John, and Zechariah, unable to speak, wrote down on a tablet, "His name is John." Immediately, his mouth was opened, and he blessed God. Then, being filled with the Holy Spirit, he prophesied. This prophecy is called the Song of Zechariah (also known as *Benedictus*, the first word in the Latin translation, which means "blessed"). In this song, Zechariah sang about fulfillment of the messianic hope that God would liberate God's people from the hands of the enemies and lead them to the life of holiness and righteousness.

The song makes a close connection between what God has already begun (1:68-75) and what God will fulfill (1:78-79). Christian hope is deeply rooted in the Jewish traditions of David's kingship (1:69), prophecy of liberation (1:70–71), and Abraham's covenant (1:72-73). The readers of Luke later learn that in Christ the meaning of being children of Abraham was expanded to include all Gentiles (Acts 3:25). Christians do not replace the Israelites, but they are grafted to Israel's history in Christ (cf. Galatians 3:6-18).

Luke contrasts "the hand of the Lord" that was with the baby John the Baptist (1:66) with the "hand of all who hate us" (1:71) and "hands of our enemies" (1:74). John Wesley thought that the hand of the Lord signifies "the peculiar power and blessing of God" (*ENNT*). Indeed, in Christian traditions, the hand of God (*manus dei*), especially the right hand of the Lord (*dextera domini*), represented God's guidance, deliverance, and protection. In early Christian art, you can see a small hand in a painting indicating the powerful presence of the invisible God. In prayer, we stretch out our hands to God, and God stretches the divine hand to us. God holds our hands as a sign of God's blessing and presence (Psalm 73:23), and we pray together with our brothers and sisters in Christ, holding their hands as a sign of our love and solidarity.

Luke presented Zechariah's song as a prophecy. When God finally opened his mouth, Zechariah, filled with the Holy Spirit, began to sing. It reminds me of the moment at Pentecost when Jesus's disciples began to speak upon the coming of the Spirit (Acts 2). When Zechariah was in doubt, his mouth was shut. When the Holy Spirit was with him, he not only regained his own voice but also spoke the words of God. However, the inspired speech was not free from forms and structures. It begins in the form of a Jewish blessing and appears to be modeled after other biblical songs and prayers. Throughout this song, Zechariah maintains his role as a speaker. Here we see another example of psalms and prayers in the Bible being presented both as human speech and as the inspired words of God. The lyrics of *Benedictus* are both Zechariah's and the Holy Spirit's words. In this song, divine and human agency do not compete with each other; they are not mutually exclusive. When we are filled with the Holy Spirit, we can find our own words of prayer are not just ours; they are also God's words given to us. Again, we can see the mysterious work of the triune God on both the divine and human sides of prayer.

Zechariah prophesied that "the dawn from on high will break upon us" (1:78). In the Christian liturgical tradition, the sunrise represents Christ. So, early Christians prayed toward the east, the direction of the sunrise, as a gesture of receiving the true light in their anticipation of Jesus's promised second coming. Zechariah's song about "the dawn from on high" has been a principal part of the church's traditional daily morning prayer. With the Song of Mary, or *Magnificat* (Luke 1:46-55), in evening prayer and the Song of Simeon, *Nunc Dimittis* (Luke 2:29-32) in night prayer, Luke's three canticles on Jesus's birth are staples of the daily liturgy of the church. Therefore, our remembrance of the Messiah's coming and anticipation of his second coming, represented in those three songs, are not limited to Advent; they are the recurring themes of daily prayers throughout the year.

Likewise, the Psalms and canticles in the Bible have been a backbone of Christian prayer in both communal liturgy and private devotion. They passionately express the whole gamut of emotions, including joy, sorrow, anger, fear, and surprise. Thus, John Calvin called the Book of Psalms "an Anatomy of all the Parts of the Soul" in the preface to his *Commentary on the Psalms*.[1] Reading or singing those ancient prayers is like looking in a mirror. The emotions of psalmists deeply resonate with us. Through the inspired words, we not only learn to express our hearts better but also discover the hidden layers of our own emotions. I remember many moments of surprise when the depth of my anger, joy, and anguish was suddenly revealed to me through the words of Psalms. In those prayers of the Scriptures, we encounter both God and ourselves, trusting that the Holy Spirit who inspired the psalmists would also refresh, remold, and reawaken our hearts.

English is my second language. I began to study it in middle school in a non-English-speaking country. When you learn a new language from a textbook, you have limited exposure to only certain genres. So, I learned how to write academic papers in English before learning how to talk with friends. Later, when I led an English-speaking congregation, I realized that I did not have the English language of prayer in me. How would I lead congregational prayer? How would I bless a child? How would I pray for healing at a hospital? How would I do all these pastoral works of prayer if I constantly search for the next words? So, I heavily borrowed words from other prayers. I memorized bits of Psalms and liturgical prayers and practiced them until they became my own words. This new experience made me highly conscious of what kind of words we use in prayer and how we use our bodies in our prayer. Growing up in a church where spontaneous shouting was the most popular form of prayer, I had never thought about how the words of prayer would shape me. We were more concerned about expressing ourselves; we rarely talked about how those words of prayer might transform us. I eventually became a scholar of Christian prayer. Now, I teach my students and congregations how our prayer not only shows but also shapes our beliefs. Language can both limit and liberate us; I came to understand Martin Heidegger's famous claim, "Language is the house of Being."[2] Language shapes us, so learning multiple languages is helpful to understand the peculiarities of different cultures. I believe learning how to pray is like learning a different language; it involves acquiring a different view of God, self, church, and world.

We can learn how to pray by borrowing words from the church's prayers: the Lord's Prayer, Psalms, canticles, and liturgy. Those borrowed words become ours, and they eventually become who we are. Those who are experienced in prayer not only have acquired good habits of prayers but have been transformed by those words. Tertullian, a theologian of the early church, famously wrote that Christians are made, not born. For early Christians, to teach how to pray was to teach how to be a Christian. The catechism of the early church usually consisted of two basic structures: the Ten Commandments and the Lord's Prayer. They became Christians by learning how to pray the Lord's Prayer, and they waited until their baptism to recite it in public worship because baptism affirmed and declared that they were God's children, who could call God "our Father."

John Wesley on Prayer

Traditionally, the church's liturgy has been called the "school of prayer" (*scola orandi*). Prayer is the school for our learning and spiritual and emotional growth. John Wesley explained how much we are transformed in our prayer:

> The end of your praying is not to inform God, as though he knew not your wants already; but rather to inform yourselves; to fix the…sense of your continual dependence on him who only is able to supply all your wants. (SSM)

A leader of this school is not necessarily a learned scholar. The community of faith recognizes the spiritual authority of faithful nonglamorous people who are committed to the life of prayer and bear the fruits of wisdom and virtues in their mundane lives. Also, this learning in the "school of prayer" does not always depend on human language. Words can express our thoughts and desires; they can also shape and edify us; but words eventually fail us too. Silence does not replace our words in prayer, but silent prayer begins where our words crumble. In silence, we open ourselves to God's presence and listen to the voices of the triune God mysteriously working in our prayer.

John Wesley lived through a watershed moment in the history of Christian prayer. Previously, using prayer books was celebrated as a means to tap the great reservoir of theological knowledge and wisdom of the church. Those written prayers were seen as a way to be spiritually united with the larger Christian communities, both diachronic (the communities of saints throughout history) and synchronic (the contemporary communities around the world). But the rising Romanticism elevated spontaneity as the genuine sign of the spirit of prayer, condemning liturgical prayers as "dead words." This new trend, which might be more familiar to us now, was a radical departure from the past practices. Spontaneity was now seen as a unique window to our true hearts.

Such new focus on individual spontaneous responses led to extra scrutiny of the heart. People soon realized how difficult it was to keep their spontaneous reactions fresh, and the reality raised a serious question for advocates of spontaneity: "How shall we translate a succession of ephemeral moments into an enduring character?" The difficulty in transition from transient spontaneity to an enduring moral character challenged the assumption that those who had the genuine experience of emotional effusion would naturally achieve moral integrity. I think this question is very relevant to us who live in the so-called age of authenticity, in which the new generation likes to locate spiritual authenticity in individuals' hearts and actions, not in the tradition.

John Wesley was one of the early evangelicals who observed this seismic shift of cultural expectations on spontaneity and authenticity. On the one hand, he agreed with the advocates of prayer books, who charged that extempore prayers were not truly free from forms and patterns. Wesley criticized Quakers who wanted to get rid of formality in both private and public prayer. Quakers believed that the set structures of formal worship would prevent the Spirit from working freely, but Wesley argued that even their prayers, supposedly free from any forms, developed a pattern in repetition, so he wrote, "I myself find more life in the Church Prayers, than in any *formal extemporary* prayers of Dissenters" (*Works* 13:34, italics mine). Indeed, Wesley's spiritual practice in his early days in Oxford Holy Club adopted the traditional liturgical practices. The Holy Club members spent an hour every morning and evening in private prayer and prayed in a group three times a week. They followed traditional hours of prayer (morning, noon, afternoon), reading from the Book of Common Prayer, Apostolic Traditions, and other devotional resources of his time. Wesley also published his very first book, Collection of Forms of Prayer for Every Day in the Week, which consisted of daily morning and evening prayers. These written prayers emphasized Christian virtues, such as humility, charity, and purity. Later, during his time in Georgia, Wesley strictly kept this practice of using prayer books.

But in April 1738, he decided not to confine himself to the forms of prayer. He tried extempore prayer for private devotion and later for public worship as well. In his letter to Samuel Walker in 1755, Wesley said that even in the church, he did not confine himself wholly to the forms of prayer, frequently adding extempore prayer before or after his sermon. Wesley was under the influence of Pietism, more particularly, Moravians, who emphasized the transformation of the heart through fervent and emotional preaching and extempore prayer. This decision put Wesley at odds with the leaders of the Church of England, including his older brother, Samuel Wesley. Believing that the Holy Spirit worked among his followers in this new practice, John Wesley argued he could not find any biblical and ecclesial laws against it. Wesley concluded that it was his "bounden duty" to introduce extempore prayer into the spiritual life of the people called Methodists. Wesley rightly recognized that the rigorous practice of extempore prayers was important for his movement's vitality, which was particularly evident in early Methodist women's prayer life. Sarah Crosby was well known for her simple, candid prayer in the Spirit. Ann Cutler, called "Praying Nanny," was praised for her intense and lengthy practice of private prayers. Many early Methodists were the less educated, the poor, or the working class; their prayers might not be elegant or sophisticated, but John Wesley was deeply touched by their often fragmentary but genuine prayers.

However, it does not mean that Wesley discarded the forms of prayer. He kept publishing the collections of prayers for his followers (*A Collection of Prayers for Families and Prayers for Children*), which again emphasized Christian virtues, confession of sins, and purity of the heart. He saw the new expression of piety would not replace but complement the traditional "school of prayer." Wesley's vision of prayerful life had two wings: the rubric of prayer books, which gave a structure to the life of holiness, and fervent extempore prayer, which allowed his new movement to have spontaneous, often explosive, outpourings of emotions. Wesley envisioned that our spiritual growth would be supported by both wings, but his Methodists quickly lost the first wing, mostly relying on the second one only.

Prayer and Sanctification

One day when I was rereading Emily Brontë's novel, *Wuthering Heights*, I stumbled upon something I had not noticed before. The main narrator, Nelly Dean, describes the dramatic moment when Heathcliff stormed into his chamber upon the news of his beloved Catherine Earnshaw's death.

> There he has continued, praying like a methodist: only the deity he implored is senseless dust and ashes; and God, when addressed, was curiously confounded with his own black father! After concluding these precious orisons—and they lasted generally till he grew hoarse and his voice was strangled in his throat—he would be off again; always straight down to the Grange![3]

He prayed like a Methodist! For a scholar of Christian prayer, it is an intriguing glimpse at an outsider's view of the Methodist practice of prayer in nineteenth-century England. In this short section, Brontë deftly highlights the exotic and foreign nature of

Heathcliff by associating him with the otherness of Methodists in the English society of her time. What did she mean by "pray[ing] like a methodist"? By the fact that Heathcliff's voice became hoarse, we can guess that Dean referred to the fervent prayer of wailing and shouting. That was the popular image of the Methodist: emotive spontaneous prayer, often associated with physical movements, such as kneeling, falling down, and dancing. Such practices resonated with farmers, factory workers, and servants, who found their space in the budding movement. Blacks (slaves and free), drawn by Methodists' antislavery views, also found such practice of prayer liberating. Soon, such fervent spontaneous prayer became the practice of Methodists, leaving Wesley's balancing work behind.

If you said, "They pray like Methodists," what would you mean by it? Most people might be interested in their distinctive style of prayer. But I think what makes the Methodist practice unique is their theological vision rather than their style. Wesley was more interested in the fruit of the Spirit that our works of piety would bear. Thus, in his sermon "Catholic Spirit," he refused to pick a single superior method of prayer: "It appears to me that forms of prayer are of excellent use, particularly in the great congregation. If you judge extemporary prayer to be of more use, act suitably to your own judgment" (SCS, 2:90). What Wesley focused on was to make their prayers be the prayers of the heart. No matter what style we may use, prayer should be a practice of discovering and reshaping our desires and developing moral characters. Behind this vision was Wesley's doctrine of Christian perfection or entire sanctification.

In our contemporary society, in which perfectionism encroaches on us everywhere, perfection might be a precarious thing to preach. The idea that a human being can be perfect sounds arrogant, if not delusional. Every youth minister I know is wrestling with rising anxiety and depression among the youth who daily struggle to meet unreasonable expectations: perfect scores, perfect portfolio, perfect body, and so on. To be honest, the doctrine of Christian perfection was the biggest hurdle for me to affirm my identity as a Wesleyan theologian. So, I *perfectly* understand why you might be uncomfortable with the language of perfection.

But my own discomfort melted away once I understood what Wesley's doctrine of Christian perfection truly meant. In fact, this doctrine now makes me excited about the Wesleyan way of making disciples of Christ. Not surprisingly, Wesley himself was constantly misunderstood and criticized for the word *perfection*. So, he had to keep clarifying what he really meant by Christian perfection. He did not mean that we would be perfect in knowledge or free from ignorance or error. We would not be wholly free from temptation either. Perfection is not the kind of goal that we can reach once and claim as ours afterward. Instead, it is a kind of goal we should constantly stay in; otherwise we would easily fall off from it. Christian perfection is like flying a kite. There is no single moment when a kite accomplishes the art of flying. Flying a kite is not like flying an airplane, which uses its own power, or putting a satellite in orbit. However perfectly it flies, the kite cannot fly by itself. It should be constantly lifted up by the wind. Once the wind is gone, it immediately falls down. Likewise, in Christian perfection, we can fly only by the support of the wind of the Holy Spirit. It is not an achieved goal, but rather it is like being in the zone with the Holy Spirit.

If he had to qualify its meaning this much, why did Wesley insist that we must strive for perfection? He thought it was a divine commandment: "Be ye therefore perfect, even as your Father which is in heaven is perfect" (Matthew 5:48 KJV). Moreover, from a more pastoral perspective, he believed keeping our eyes on Christian perfection as a telos of our Christian life is necessary for our long journey of discipleship. Once we lose the goal, it is difficult to sustain the daily (mostly mundane) works of Christian life: works of piety and works of mercy. Over the decades of his successful ministry, Wesley still saw so many of his beloved friends, colleagues, and followers who were once greatly moved by the Holy Spirit and pledged to work together to spread scriptural holiness backsliding and disappearing from the community. He lamented that many once-thriving Methodist societies were almost gone by the next time he visited them, losing their shared zeal for spiritual practices. As a seasoned pastor, Wesley knew how important the routine practices of the means of grace are for our spiritual growth. Even an extraordinary manifestation of the power of the Spirit would not carry us far enough without our participation in ordinary practices. And without sharing this hope of sanctification, Wesley thought, most people likely lose their fervor and regress to their former selves before awakening. And later, looking back on the history of the Methodist movement, he worried that many Methodists had lost sight of this blessing of Christian perfection and consequently suffered from backsliding. So, Wesley kept preaching the doctrine of Christian perfection until the end of his life, believing "God has peculiarly entrusted [it] to the Methodists" (JD, February 2, 1789).

I explained what Wesley did not mean by Christian perfection. But then, what is perfection? Perfection is none other than life in love, a life so saturated in love that all our thoughts and actions are overflow from love. "The loving God with all our heart, mind, soul, and strength. This implies no wrong temper, none contrary to love, remains in the soul; and that all the thoughts, words, and actions are governed by pure love" (PCP).

You might wonder why I am reiterating the importance of the doctrine of Christian perfection in this chapter on prayer. In addition to the fact that this doctrine is so essential to understanding Wesley's vision of Christian life, prayer has a unique place in our journey toward entire sanctification. Prayer is not only the means of grace that leads us toward perfection, but in union with God we live in perfection itself. We can see this point in Wesley's commentary on 1 Thessalonians 5:16–18, "Rejoice evermore. Pray without ceasing. In every thing give thanks: for this is the will of God in Christ Jesus concerning you" (KJV). Wesley saw these three practices essentially interconnected; praying without ceasing is "the fruit of always rejoicing in the Lord," and giving thanks in everything is the fruit of both "uninterrupted happiness in God" and unceasing prayer (ENNT). When they continually enkindle one another in our life, we experience entire sanctification.

In this description of incessant prayer in perfection, Wesley called prayer "the breath of spiritual life." When we mature on our spiritual journey, we get to see that prayer is no longer our intermittent action but being in constant communion with God. God's Spirit breathes into us, and we breathe back into God in our prayer. God's breath of life is closer to us than our own breath. He explained this spiritual reparations more in his sermon "New Birth":

> God is continually breathing, as it were, upon the soul; and his soul is breathing unto God. Grace is descending into his heart; and prayer and praise ascending to heaven. (SNB, 2:193)

God always breathes into us first. God initiates and sustains this intimate loving relationship. But we have to breathe back in prayer to stay in this loving relationship. In our prayer, we learn to discern, trust, and follow God's will. In our prayer, our words, thoughts, and actions become saturated in divine love, and we gradually become love itself. This is the vision of Wesleyan spirituality.

But not everyone liked the people called Methodists. Many privileged people of eighteenth-century England accused them of disrupting the social and ecclesial establishments. When Methodist preachers came to a town, a great multitude came to listen to them, but also a mob came to throw stones at them. In defense of his people, John Wesley wrote a treatise titled "The Character of a Methodist" (1742), in which he explained that the distinguishing "marks of a Methodist" were not their different theological opinions or ecclesial policies, but their commitment to spiritual discipline and their transformed hearts filled with love of God and love of neighbor. He named praying without ceasing as one of those marks of being a Methodist.

Wesley admitted that Methodists did not remain in the house of worship or pray on their knees all the time, even though they did so as much as possible. By "praying without ceasing," Wesley meant that one's heart would always say, "Thou brightness of the eternal glory, unto thee is my heart, though without a voice, and my silence speaketh unto thee." He called this language of the heart "true prayer." As long as they lived a life of Christian perfection in their rejoicing, praying, and giving thanks, Methodists would always remain in love with God and in love with their neighbor. The greatest commandment ("love your God and love your neighbor") is "written in [their] heart." And this love extends to every human being, every child of God, so Methodists do not stop praying for everyone, including their enemies. Love purifies their hearts so that they will have the mind of Christ and fix their eyes on God.

What is so interesting to me about this treatise is that Wesley did not say he hoped Methodists would pray without ceasing. He rather declared as a matter of fact that this was who a Methodist was. He defined Methodists as those who delve into the spiritual practices and reach to the stage of unceasing prayer and hence Christian perfection. I rarely see such a high expectation for Methodists or other Christians nowadays. How could Wesley be so optimistic about the people called Methodists? It was not because he trusted his people in particular or humanity in general. He was as skeptical as any of us could be about our innate capacity to be holy. But Wesley had a great faith in God, who works in, for, and with us. He believed when we entrust ourselves to God's sanctifying grace, our experience of perfection can happen on earth. It is not a remote goal, never available for us here and now.

Incarnation and Sanctification

God makes our transformation possible. This is the prominent theme of the Advent season. What did Jesus accomplish in his incarnation? With the Nicene Creed, we confess, "For us and for our salvation [Christ] came down from heaven, was incarnate of the Holy Spirit and the Virgin Mary and became truly human." Christ's incarnation was not merely a rite of passage toward his crucifixion. The purpose of the Incarnation should not be reduced to his death. The Incarnation touches the ontological (about our nature) aspect of our salvation. Gregory of Nazianzus, a fourth-century theologian, famously said, "What has not been assumed has not been healed; it is what is united to his divinity that is saved."[4] It means Christ, fully divine and fully human, assumed and transformed the whole human nature for our salvation. Christ made our sanctification possible, not only by empowering us to do the right things but also restoring our human nature itself. By becoming a human being, Christ opened the possibility for us to be like him. Elsewhere, Gregory wrote, "Let us be like Christ, because Christ became like us. Let us become gods through him since he himself, through us, became a man. He took the worst upon himself to make us a gift of the best."[5]

Theologians call this idea of becoming like Christ the doctrine of deification, or *theosis* (literally meaning "making divine"). It does not mean that we become God or demi-god. It means by the grace of God, we can partake in the divine nature and become holy. Such theology of deification is prominent in Eastern Orthodox teachings, but we can find a similar idea in the Wesley brothers' writings on Christian perfection. John Wesley's definition of salvation includes the restoration of our soul and the recovery of the divine nature: "By salvation I mean…a present deliverance from sin, a restoration of the soul to its primitive health, its original purity; a recovery of the divine nature…. This implies all holy and heavenly tempers, and by consequence all holiness of conversation" (*Farther Appeal*, pt. I, §3). Charles Wesley's Christmas hymns sing about this doctrine of deification against the background of Christ's incarnation.

Before looking at Charles Wesley's *Nativity Hymns* (1745), let's meditate on the so-called Christ Hymn in the Epistle to Philippians.

Let the same mind be in you that was in Christ Jesus,

> *who, though he was in the form of God,*
>   *did not regard equality with God*
>   *as something to be exploited,*
> *but emptied himself,*
>   *taking the form of a slave,*
>   *being born in human likeness.*
> *And being found in human form,*
>   *he humbled himself*
>   *and became obedient to the point of death—*
>   *even death on a cross.*

> *Therefore God also highly exalted him*
>   *and gave him the name*
>   *that is above every name,*
> *so that at the name of Jesus*
>   *every knee should bend,*
>   *in heaven and on earth and under the earth,*
> *and every tongue should confess*
>   *that Jesus Christ is Lord,*
>   *to the glory of God the Father.*
>   *Philippians 2:5-11*

A similar image of Christ's incarnation can be found in Charles Wesley's Hymn 5 in *Nativity Hymns*.

> Glory be to God on high,
> And peace on earth descend;
> God comes down: he bows the sky:
> And shews himself our friend!
> God th' invisible appears,

> God the blest, the great I AM
> Sojourns in this vale of tears,
> And Jesus is his name.

In the second stanza, he echoed the language of emptying (*kenosis*) and sang about the paradox that the source of Being itself was born in history.

> Emptied of his majesty,
> Of his dazling glories shorn,
> Being's source *begins* to be,
> And God himself is BORN!

And he added a little, but significant, phrase to the idea of emptying: "Empty'd of all but love he came" (Hymn 15). In an earlier hymn, he also sang, "He left his throne above / Emptied of all, but love" ("Hymn on the Titles of Christ," *Hymns and Sacred Poems* 1739, 167). Love is the very essence of God, so "Love Divine, all loves excelling" can never empty of love without stopping being God. In love and as love, Christ came to earth to be with us. God's presence in Christ came to us as a surprising gift, unfathomable grace. Christ's being with us not only made invisible God visible to us but also made our ontological transformation possible. By the Incarnation, Christ assumed the whole humanity and transformed our nature, so that we could become like Christ. Charles Wesley expressed this vision in Hymn 5 of *Nativity Hymns*.

> He deigns in flesh t' appear,
> Widest extremes to join,

To bring our vileness near,
And make us all divine;
And we the life of God shall know,
For God is manifest below.

Made perfect first in love,
And sanctified by grace,
We shall from earth remove,
And see his glorious face;
His love shall then be fully shew'd,
And man shall all be lost in God.

As I said previously, Christ's "mak[ing] us all divine" does not mean we literally become God. Rather, it means we participate in Christ, becoming holy and being made perfect in love. This vision was shared in the following lyrics of Charles Wesley's hymns:

What mov'd the Most High so greatly to stoop,
He comes from the sky our souls to lift up;
That sinners forgiven, might sinless return
To God and to Heaven; their Maker is born.
(Hymn 7)

The Ancient of Days
To redeem a lost race,
From his glory comes down,
Self-humbled to carry us up to a crown.

Made flesh for our sake,
That we might partake
The nature divine,

72

And again in his image, his holiness shine
(Hymn 8)

A peace on earth he brings,
Which never more shall end:
The Lord of hosts, the King of kings,
Declare himself our friend,
Assumes our flesh and blood
That we his Sp'rit may gain"
(Hymn 9)

John Wesley explained our partaking in divine nature not as something we possess but as a loving relationship with God. It is not about who we are as independent beings; it is about who we are in our relationship with God. We are drawn into "a deep, an intimate, an uninterrupted union with God; a constant communion with the Father and his Son Jesus Christ, through the Spirit; a continual enjoyment of the Three-One God, and of all the creatures in [God]!" (SNC). Our incessant prayer is a foretaste of this "uninterrupted union with God." From this larger perspective of Christian perfection or entire sanctification, prayer is much more than repeating our wish lists; it is both a way toward perfection and a blessed experience of it.

Prayer and Love of Neighbor

We never pray alone, even when we enter a closet and pray alone in secret. We are united with other people as well as Christ and Holy Spirit in our prayers. When we recite the Lord's Prayer, we pray as "we" (a community), not as isolated individuals. In our prayers, we are all connected to one another in the Spirit. We pray for the entire world because we care about others. Prayer is not escapism. When we pray, "Thy kingdom come," we dream about the transformation of the world. God's kingdom is coming to us, instead of us escaping this world. We pray for God's perfect reign of God, in which God's righteousness and justice overflow. In prayer, we are nudged, pushed, and propelled to participate in God's mission in the world. In this Advent season, I invite you to ponder the prophetic messages in Mary's, Zechariah's, and Simeon's songs in the Gospel of Luke. Those songs or prayers remind us that our prayer must not be a docile acceptance of the evil reality. In Christ, the world would be turned upside down. The rich, the powerful, and the proud will be humbled, but the lowly, the poor, and the hungry will be satisfied. The light of God, which expels darkness and brings us peace, has been revealed to all nations and all people, crossing all kinds of boundaries that have divided us.

Likewise, our prayer, inspired by the Holy Spirit, raises a prophetic voice. If our prayer does not lead us to meaningful actions, we should ask ourselves whether we are praying right. When I see people saying, "My prayers are with you" but refusing to take actions about our broken world, I cannot but wonder what kind of prayer they offer to God. I would ask why prayer inspired by the Spirit of God would not make us deeply engage in the world.

I understand people become frustrated with the lack of responsible actions of those who call for prayer. I understand when they say, "I am tired of prayer." However, I think separating prayer from action creates a false dichotomy. The problem of inaction does not lie in prayer itself; a right kind of prayer is a profound action that challenges us to do right things. The problem is a superficial or false understanding of prayer. Prayer is not empty rhetorical gestures or paying lip service to certain abstract causes, which I consider a theological malpractice. Instead, we go through profound moments of transformation through our prayers of confession, lamentation, thanksgiving, and petition. The "school of prayer" is a spiritual place where such a radical reorientation and transformation of a self happens. For me, prayer is a school, gymnasium, and home, where shaping, reshaping, nurturing, and practicing constantly take place. Those who are trained in this school cannot but hear and answer God's call for righteousness and mercy.

As a teacher, pastor, parent, and friend, I often ask people, "How may I pray for you?" To answer this question, most people hasten to come up with something beyond their control. If they do not find anything urgent, they say, "Nothing special." I rarely see people sharing their vision and hope for sanctification in their prayer requests. How may I pray for those people? I often begin with Paul's words in Ephesians.

> *I pray that the God of our Lord Jesus Christ, the Father of glory, may give you a spirit of wisdom and revelation as you come to know him, so that, with the eyes of your heart enlightened, you may know what is the hope to which he has called you, what*

*are the riches of his glorious inheritance among the
saints, and what is the immeasurable greatness of his
power for us who believe.*

Ephesians 1:17-19a

What kind of intercessory prayer did he have for the church in Ephesus? It is certainly not a list of crisis. Instead, it is a list of blessings, which capture the Christian dream of sanctification. To nudge people to imagine who we could be in prayer, I ask different questions now: "How may I bless you in my prayers?" or "How may I pray for your spiritual growth?" Then I lavishly blessed them in my prayers. Praying for others literally means giving your life to others, because the time you spend in intercessory prayer is your life itself. When you pray for others, you are sharing your life with them. That's why it is so hard to pray for someone you do not love. But we still try to pray for our enemies because we want to love them. It is difficult to hate someone you just profusely blessed, spending your precious time. I do not mean that blessing others will automatically fix our broken relationships; it would not be wise to rush for blessing, ignoring injustice and harm done by offenders. There should be always a place for lamentation and supplication for justice in our prayers. But divine love ultimately leads us to love of our neighbor, and our intercessory prayer, I believe, is one of the greatest expressions of that love.

We Pray Because We Love

Why do we pray? There are many different motivations for our prayers. We might pray out of the sense of duty or the fear of losing an opportunity. But my favorite answer is "We pray because we love!" God loved us first, reaching out to us for a loving relationship, and in response, we pray, seeking a constant communion with God. We can boldly pray because Christ, who emptied himself and came to us, understands our agony, unbelief, and frustration and stands with us as our mediator. We can express doubts, raise questions, or protest because we have deep trust in God's goodness, revealed to us in Christ's incarnation. We pray for others because we share God's love with all our neighbors regardless of their different backgrounds.

What would it mean for us to pray like a Methodist? Praying without ceasing, with relentless hope and trust in God's promise of sanctification, is a mark of Wesleyan spirituality. In this Advent, I invite you to remember what Christ has done for us in his incarnation and what he has promised to fulfill in us. Christ, who emptied of all but love, became a human to make us become like him. Christ has made the impossible possible, so in prayer, we partake in Christ's divine nature. Let us pray for this journey toward entire sanctification. Because of Christ's incarnation, we can seek the perfect union with God in our prayers. Christ has come to us as Emmanuel, "God is with us" (Matthew 1:23). Hear this good news of Advent in John Wesley's last words on earth: "Best of all, God is with us."

Prayer

Ah, Lord!—if thou art in that sigh,
Then hear thyself within me pray.

Hear in my heart thy Spirit's cry,
Mark what my labouring soul would say,
Answer the deep, unuttered groan,
And show that thou and I are one.[6]

Love Divine, all loves excelling,
Come to our hearts, and teach us how to pray.
Hear our prayers of love.
Open our ears to hear your voice.
Help us to partake in your glory.
Transform our hearts to be made perfect in love.
Make us united with you in our prayers.
We pray in the name of Jesus, Love Incarnate, Amen.

Chapter Three

Practices of Mercy

Embodying God's Love for Others

JUNG CHOI

In my room, I have a print of *The Annunciation* by Henry Ossawa Tanner (1859–1937). This painting is simply exquisite: in a closed room, adorned with beautiful red cloth, an adolescent Mary faces Gabriel, who is portrayed as light. Her two hands gathered in her lap, her face tilted, Mary is attentive and engaged. Her bright eyes simultaneously show her audacity, curiosity, and fear.[1]

Christmas stories feature Mary in her encounter with God. Gabriel has just told her that a child would be borne through her, and the baby, Jesus, will save the world. She accepts God's invitation and sings the song of Mary, which is called the *Magnificat*, coming from the first word in the Latin translation.

> *"My soul magnifies the Lord,*
> > *and my spirit rejoices in God my Savior,*
> *for he has looked with favor on the lowliness of his servant.*
> > *Surely, from now on all generations will call me blessed;*
> *for the Mighty One has done great things for me,*
> > *and holy is his name.*
> *His mercy is for those who fear him*
> > *from generation to generation.*
> *He has shown strength with his arm;*
> > *he has scattered the proud in the thoughts of their hearts.*
> *He has brought down the powerful from their thrones,*
> > *and lifted up the lowly;*
> *he has filled the hungry with good things,*
> > *and sent the rich away empty.*
> *He has helped his servant Israel,*
> > *in remembrance of his mercy,*
> *according to the promise he made to our ancestors,*
> > *to Abraham and to his descendants forever."*
> > > *Luke 1:46b-55*

God's Agency and Power over Human Lives

Here we see God's incredible power that saves people throughout time. Simultaneously, we see Mary's agency that obeys God's amazing power. God's agency and power are manifest. God chooses Mary to be a receptacle of Jesus (Luke 1:31: "And now, you will conceive in your womb and bear a son, and you will name him Jesus"). The thrust of Gabriel's overall message is that nothing is impossible with God. What God expects from Mary is unthinkable, which no human being can fathom. When Mary asks, "How can this be, since I am a virgin?" (Luke 1:34), the angel Gabriel did not fully answer her question but replied simply, "The Holy Spirit will come upon you, and the power of the Most High will overshadow you" (Luke 1:35). The answer is vague at best. Neither Mary nor any other human being could fully understand what Gabriel told her. God's power is shrouded in mystery.

We also see that God's will and power could be perceived as violent, for God's plan is imposed upon Mary's life in such a surprising way. God's breaking in Mary's life forever changed her life. In this way, Mary situates herself as a "servant of the Lord" in her song (Luke 1:38). It is noteworthy that the word translated here as *servant* (*doulos*) literally means "slave." This is not a romantic or idealized concept that some modern readings would like to provide.

God's agency is also expressed from the syntax of these sentences. We see that God is the subject of verses 48-55: God has looked with favor; God has shown great strength; God has scattered the proud; God has brought down the powerful; God has lifted up the lowly; God has filled the hungry with good things.

God has sent the rich away empty; God made the promise to our ancestors, which amplifies the work of God, who is in control of our lives. It is also noteworthy that these verbs are given in the past tense, which reflects the everlasting truth. Put differently, according to Fred Craddock in his commentary on Luke, what God did in this song is true across time: past, present, and future.[2]

Mary's Agency: Her Bold Obedience

While we see God's power and mystery in this story, we also see an amazing agency by Mary. She is not a passive being who just receives God's message. She actively proclaims, "Here am I, the servant of the Lord; let it be with me according to your word" (Luke 1:38). Mary expresses her amazing feat of obedience when she says yes, while she would imagine what kinds of repercussions would be laid bare in her life because of her obedience. Her obedience is not a mere resignation of her will. Rather, Mary exercises her will and agency to accept God's plan in her life, even though it might be forever changing the course of her life. Mary's obedience to God's will in her life—to have a baby through the Spirit—is a fierce one: It is not for the faint of heart. In a world colonized by the Roman Empire, to be a woman in such a society was really hard on so many levels. She could have imagined that there would be gossip and misunderstanding about her. In this way, Mary's obedience and faithfulness serve as a model for many people of God who come after her. This fierce and bold obedience must have come from her relationship with God, her trust in God, who leads and takes care of God's people as God promised. We see again and again how Mary's special status is elevated by her obedience and attentiveness to the words of God. When Mary and Joseph brought a twelve-year-old Jesus to the Jerusalem Temple during Passover—as they had done every year—other people did not understand when Jesus said, "Why you were searching for me? Did you not know that I must be in my Father's house?" (Luke 2:49). It was Mary who "treasured all these things in her heart" (Luke 2:51b). In Luke 11:27-28, a woman in the crowd shouts out to Jesus, "Blessed is the womb that bore and the breasts that nursed you!" To this woman's cry, Jesus returns and reorganizes her view by saying, "Blessed rather are those who hear the word of God and obey it!" Luke shows that Mary is blessed by her obedience and relationship with God, rather than by her biological birth of Jesus. Her bold obedience is shown in many as we shall see in many faithful people of God in the following sections.

The Magnificat: God's Vision for the Marginalized and the Poor

Mary is portrayed to be the ideal disciple through her bold obedience and hereafter extols God's marvelous acts with prophecy and vision. This prophecy and vision are connected to God's mercy on everyone, especially on the marginalized, the lowly, and the poor. In the political and social situation of Mary and her people, who were suffering under the colonization of the Roman Empire, the prophecy is particularly great news. Mary prophesies the great act and mercy of God, which breaks the barriers and spreads God's justice and liberation for people. We see here God's mighty power is ingrained in *eleos* (1:54, 58, 72, 78), a Greek word that denotes compassion and mercy to the unfortunate and the poor. It is also the Greek translation of the Hebrew (*hesed*)—as the Old Testament/Hebrew Bible was written in Hebrew, while the New Testament was written in Greek—which adds on the layer of faithfulness, a mutual relationship.

The vision that we see in the Magnificat is not merely a dream for a distant future or the end time (*eschaton*), when Christ comes back to judge the quick and the dead. Instead, the vision has already occurred due to Jesus's coming to the world, for throughout his life, Jesus's ministry reflected the vision that Mary prophecies about— the lowly and the humiliated people become exalted, which Luke's Gospel repeatedly underscores. This vision is also not to be pigeonholed as spiritual or otherworldly, in the sense that it lacks the concrete daily engagement with God's world. For Luke offers, "Blessed are you who are poor, for yours is the kingdom of God" (Luke 6:20), while Matthew says, "Blessed are the poor in spirit, for theirs is the kingdom of heaven" (Matthew 5:3). The difference between these two texts adds nuance to the Magnificat, which proclaims God's mercy for the lowly and the poor. On the contrary, Mary's vision is ingrained with contemporary worldly matters. We see from Luke's Gospel the constant message that the culmination may be fully realized in the future, but salvation comes here and now in the present day. For Mary and her people, the coming of the

Savior (Messiah, Christ) certainly has an impact on present human affairs: when the Roman emperor considers himself as a god, Mary and her people would boldly say, "No, you are not a god. We serve one God, and our God sends the Savior for us."

Mary's Communal Vision

Mary belonged to a strong community of God's people. Joseph was a partner who was willing to take a great risk as well in his obedience to God. Elizabeth was a cousin who understood the difficulty of life as a woman, particularly a pregnant woman, at the time. In this way, communities are created with the people beyond their times. We call them the saints.

As much as Mary's song is magnificent and impressive, her song is not a solitary piece. This song is all the more powerful, with resonances coming from the previous songs and visions of many people of God—and as we shall see later, to those of many people of God in the future. On the one hand, her song is reminiscent of her older cousin Elizabeth's song—Elizabeth had conceived miraculously in spite of her advanced age. Just like Mary, Elizabeth had been visited by the angel Gabriel to prepare her for her miracle baby. Just like Mary, Elizabeth lived with gossip and probably with shame, as we could imagine from Luke 1:24. The close proximity between Mary and Elizabeth is so striking that in some ancient manuscripts, the Magnificat is attributed to Elizabeth, not Mary. Mary's song is also connected to Hannah's song, which glorifies the amazing work of the Lord (1 Samuel 2:1-10). Mary soon meets

Zechariah, whose prophecy is commensurable to her prophecy. In this way, Mary's song is inextricably connected to many years of the Israelites' history and emphasizes the loving relationship between God and human beings, and God's promise to deliver God's people from evil. Mary's song is a form of prophecy—as John Wesley also pointed out with many other theologians—which was connected to the history of Israel, through various prophets who prophesy for God's desire for the world and, most important, for Christ's salvation.

God's Vision for All the People

Mary, like many other Jewish people, yearned for the Savior (*Messiah* in Hebrew and Christ in Greek), who would deliver them from their dire situations. We remember that many people asked Jesus whether he is the One, namely, the Messiah or Christ for whom they have been waiting. Mary amplifies these yearnings of her people when she says, "[God] has helped His servant Israel, in remembrance of his mercy, according to the promise he made to our ancestors, to Abraham and to his descendants forever" (Luke 1:54-55). This is a quintessential covenant (promise) to Mary's people, Abraham's descendants. This is the hope that held Mary and her people so that they would have persevered in the midst of their harsh reality under successions of superpowers that invaded them and belittled them—the Roman Empire, the Hellenistic kingdom, the Babylonian exile, Assyria, Egypt, and so on. Their faith is genuine; their hope is solid; their yearning is warranted.

What we see missing in Mary's praise of God's covenant with Abraham and his descendants is, however, that God's covenant includes people beyond her people. We remember that in Genesis, one of the renditions on the covenants between God and Abraham reflects this theme. Genesis 17:7 ("I will establish my covenant between me and you, and your offspring after you throughout their generations, for an everlasting covenant, to be God to *you and to your offspring after you*") is expanded in Genesis 22:17-18 ("I will indeed bless you, and I will make your offspring as numerous as the stars of heaven and as the sand that is on the seashore. And your offspring shall possess the gate of their enemies, and *by your offspring shall all the nations of the earth gain blessing for themselves, because you have obeyed my voice*").

Even in the spectacular spiritual experience—in the encounter with the angel—Mary does not quite get the full scope of God's vision. This is because Mary is human, and no human being would be able to understand the scope of God's vision fully. Luke's Gospel presents Jesus, who, throughout his ministry of teaching and healing, his own death, and his resurrection, and Luke's Acts of the Apostles, the second volume of Luke's work, presents his disciples and God's people to spread the gospel in the sense that Jesus is the Savior (Messiah and Christ) for the entire world, not just the Israelite people. According to Luke, Jesus is the fulfillment of God's promise and covenant, not just for Abraham and his descendants, but also for all the people who will be blessed by Abraham (Genesis 22:18). This notion that the birth of Jesus is a blessing for everyone, not just for Mary's people, is beautifully and powerfully presented by the angels who announced and celebrated Jesus's birth. In Luke 2:10, the angels said to the shepherds, "Do not be afraid; for see—I am bringing you good news of great joy for all the people." How wonderful it is that Jesus's birth is a blessing for *all the people*, not just Mary's people!

Indeed, Mary was a bold and obedient young woman who accepted God's enigmatic message and said yes to the Lord. However, even in this wonderful act of obedience and boldness, which will be the example of faith for many people after her, we see Mary's limitation in fully fathoming God's vision for the world. This is not specific to Mary. No one would be able to understand the amazing scope and depth of God's vision for the world. It is why only angels could get it. This limitation of Mary does not discourage us from doing God's works. On the contrary, we are encouraged to do God's works with humility. Humility is required, for we may not fully understand God's vision for the entire world. We can only see the vision partially, mostly from our own perspective in relation to our people. God gradually leads us from our own understanding of salvation to God's own vision of salvation, which is for all of God's people. We are being sanctified in the sense that our points of view are being transformed into God's point of view.

In this way, Mary's story and her Magnificat also beautifully illustrate the intricate Wesleyan theology of prevenient grace, justifying grace, and sanctifying grace. Indeed, God chooses Mary, justifies her, and invites her to the journey of sanctification with God. It is God's steadfast covenant that redeems all of us who are redeemed in the name of Christ. The Wesleyan overarching theology on grace beautifully underscores the organic relationship between God and us, defying an unhelpful contrast between grace (God's agency) and human attempts. The human-divine relationship in these stories does not denote that two actors (the human and God) have equal powers in the relationship; it is clear in Mary's story that the highest and greatest actor is God. Human response to God's will is such a pivotal theme as well. This human response to God's will is always connected to the love of others. It is especially for the poor and for the marginalized, as the Magnificat shows.

John Wesley and
God's Vision for All People

In "Scripture Way of Salvation (part III. no. 10)," Wesley expounds the nature of the sanctification and the necessary "works of mercy" or "practices of mercy." In the following section, we will see some examples of those who answered God's call with bold obedience. When they say, "Here am I, the servant of the Lord; let it be with me according to your word," they witness God's wondrous and mysterious works in their lives and the world. In their works, they live out the vision of the Magnificat and Wesley's "works of mercy."

Vignette: Practice of Mercy in Our Lives

In 1903, long before Korea was divided into North and South Korea resulting from the Korean War (1950–1953), the Lucy Cuninggim Girls' School was founded by two female Southern Methodist missionaries (A. Carroll and M. Knowles) in a town called Wonsan, now in North Korea. These two female missionaries were financially supported by the North Carolina Conference Women Foreign Missionary Association, which funded the building of Lucy Cuninggim Girls' School. The school was named after Lucy Cuninggim (1838–1908), the president of the North Carolina Conference Women Foreign Missionary Association, to honor her leadership and dedication to the ministry. Another female missionary, named Hallie Buie, was the first principal of the school. According to *Women and Missions*, "The North Carolina Conference women contributed their thank offering to this enlargement of the new school and gave to the school the name Lucy Cuniggim in memory of her ministry. A beautiful location near the Korean Methodist church was selected, and a home for the missionaries and a building for the school were erected. The South Georgia Conference furnished the money, but the school retained its original name. In 1917 the total enrollment was 269."[3]

All of these women missionaries boldly said yes to God's call and followed the Spirit's guidance, leaving their homes to be on a journey to unknown places. Their relationships with God and trust in Jesus would carry them wherever they needed to go. They wanted to practice mercy for God's people. Members of the North Carolina Conference Women Foreign Missionary Association were also committed to the same vision.

My great-grandfather, one of the first Korean Methodist pastors, served as a chaplain and Bible teacher for both the Old Testament and the New Testament at the Lucy Cuninggim school for more than twenty years. He left his hometown to take the position of chaplain and Bible teacher for the students while serving at a local Korean Methodist church in partnership with American Methodist missionaries and pastors. The school was disbanded sometime after 1945—as the tension between the northern and the southern part of Korea went deeper—and the north, which would later establish the communist government, did not allow the Christian Mission school in their territory. Many of the teachers and students migrated to the south, which would later establish the government called Republic of Korea (commonly known as South Korea).

Many Korean girls were educated at the Lucy Cuninggim Girls' School who subsequently became leaders in various sectors in Korea. Some of the alumnae became teachers themselves for colleges, seminaries, and elementary schools in big cities and the disfranchised in Korea. Some of them went into business sectors. Some later went to seminaries and became pastors. Some became politicians. Many of them were deeply involved with the independent movement from the Japanese colonization, which had ruled Korea from 1910 to 1945. Just as many Koreans did, my great-grandfather and his students grappled with their realities and with the meaning of Jesus Christ in the dire political and social realities under the colonial rule by Japan.

Fast-forward sixty years. I now reside in North Carolina to teach and serve the people of God. For some years, I taught undergraduate students as a professor of religious studies at North Carolina Wesleyan College, which is affiliated with The United Methodist Church. Being at a small liberal arts college, I was "the Bible professor," teaching both the New Testament and the Old Testament to undergraduate students and second-career adult students, just as my great-grandfather taught the Bible at Lucy Cuninggim Girls' School. I also have taught graduate students who are preparing for ministry or already in the ministry setting, such as the Course of Study programs for The United Methodist Church and the Deaconess and Home Missioner at the United Methodist Women program. Soon I will also offer courses on disparate readings of the Bible from global siblings in Christ to master's students at Duke Divinity School.

My Story: I Say Yes to the Lord

God's vision works mysteriously beyond time and space. I didn't realize that it was the North Carolina Women's Society that supported and funded Lucy Cuninggim Girls' School until I moved into North Carolina from Massachusetts. We are here to serve God and to practice mercy and love. We are following the steps of many witnesses—Mary, Methodist women missionaries,

my great-grandfather, my grandmother, and countless witnesses—
who boldly obey God's call, which may destroy, reconstruct, and
rearrange our dreams. "Here we are. Let your will be done. Let us
serve you and your people."

When I got the calling of God's voice in my heart and
answered God's calling to teach and raise future pastors for God,
I was a seventeen-year-old with bright eyes just as we see Mary in
Henry Ossawa Tanner's painting. I remember my prayers when I
responded to the small voice in my heart. I recognize that it was
God with whom I had had a trusting relationship. I was pleased
and happy that God called me. My obedience was bold, and I was
thinking, *I can go anywhere God leads me. Let your will be done in
my life.* Oh, how I didn't know what kinds of journeys God would
lead me on. God has broken my plans so many times. I figuratively
found myself on the cliff many times and cried out to God, "I
thought that you called out to me to do your work. But why are
things this hard? I feel like I am drowning. Where are you? Did I
really hear your voice?"

In those moments, I remember Mary, who may have cried
out to God countless times. "Didn't you call me? Where are you?
Didn't I hear your voice? Didn't I see your presence?" But after a
moment of silence, I also remember her agency, bold obedience
again and again. "Let your will be done." I also feel connected
to A. Carroll, M. Knowles, and Lucy Cuninggim, who were
American Methodist pioneers. I feel connected to my great-
grandfather and my grandmothers, Korean Methodist pioneers.

I can imagine their cries out to God. How hard it must have been to the American Methodist pioneers to be in another, foreign land and go through difficulties. I can imagine my great-grandfather who left his hometown to take the position of chaplain in the Lucy Girls' school to educate future generations of women leaders and to educate bright young girls such as my grandmothers. I also imagine so many nameless saints throughout time and space, who boldly said to God, "Yes, I can. Yes, your will be done." Their lives have been ravaged and hard and in ways they would never have imagined. Their histories and their testimonies are here with all of us.

Humility in Practices of Mercy

In Advent, through Mary's stories, we face the complicated picture of our faith journeys. We, as people of God, tread our path with obedience and boldness. These seemingly contradictory virtues are what we see in the Magnificat. We see God, who is liberating us and yet who wants us to be God's servants. We see how God's agency and our agency are intertwined in our lives. We, as people of God, engage with this complication directly and without fear.

Our God also calls us to spread God's mercy and justice, as Mary's Magnificat extols and as Jesus would live out later. Mary's song is to upend the worldly understanding of social structure. This prayer is not good news to those who try to keep the class system and the status quo. This prayer is not like those prayers for the sake of keeping the subordinated people subordinated. God commanded the Israelites to remember that it is God who had saved them from slavery under the Egyptians. Jesus, as a Jew, celebrated the Passover, which is exactly the moment when the liberation from slavery is remembered and celebrated. Our God challenges us to do such a complicated thing. God breaks down our dreams and hopes but reconstructs our dreams and hopes to liberate and to spread mercy and justice of God in this world for the people of God.

God works mysteriously throughout times and spaces. God's steadfast love is all the more remarkable, for we all, as human beings, have our limitations. We have seen that Mary may not have realized how God's vision through Christ will affect all the people beyond the scope of her people. We might also see limitations in people of God who do God's works and practice mercies for others. Mary's song and Hannah's song encourage us not to be positioned on the side of "the proud in the thoughts of their hearts," for God "has scattered" them (Luke 1:51). They encourage us not to be positioned on the side of "the powerful from their thrones," for God "has brought down" these rulers (1:52). But in our obedience to God's call and in our practice of mercies for our sisters and brothers, we may *inadvertently* marginalize some people of God. We may *inadvertently* reinscribe our dominion upon other sisters and brothers of Christ, sustaining their subordination to us, making them "less than us." We may force our understanding of God's vision instead of God's vision on the entire world.

While missions are practices of love, the field of missions presents culturally and morally complicated pictures, with colonialism and imperialism imposed on the people by Western Christianity. Missionaries at times used to deliver Christ's gospel devoid of the cultural context of their mission field. We also see that Christian sisters and brothers wrestle with working on reconciliation and forgiveness in the midst of painful histories of war, colonialization, and violence. We also see that many Christians considered themselves specially chosen people of God, shunning reconciliation and forgiveness, thus failing to realize God's grace is for all people. In spite of these limitations, however, their faithfulness and courageous obedience are still to be admired and remembered. Those who put their lives on the line for the sake of God's vision and mercy for the world are appreciated. We all do God's works true to our own era, however limited our attempts might be.

So, we need humility in all we do—humility that recognizes that while we practice mercies in responding to God's call, we are limited; we may not fully understand God's vision for the entire world. In humility, we trust that God faithfully leads all the people of God and sanctifies all of us. As we have seen in the Magnificat (1:54, 58), *eleos* (compassion and mercy to the unfortunate and the poor) is not a unilateral action from the one with power and privilege to the less fortunate. Compassion and mercy (*eleos*) are predicated on faithfulness, which is a mutual relationship—faithfulness between God and us, and faithfulness among all the people of God. In this mutual relationship among God and all the people of God, we are invited to keep our trusting relationship with God and to keep our hope in Jesus Christ. As Mary teaches us, Christians tread our journey, accompanying our God, with obedience, carefulness, and boldness. These seemingly contradictory virtues work together in each and every one of God's people.

Fear and Yet Longing

Advent is the period of waiting and longing for the birth of Christ. The message of Advent—waiting for Jesus and his birth—is connected to the Resurrection as if it is a musical coda. In this time of the global pandemic, in this time of national and internal unrest, in this time of tremendous death and loss and grief, all of us are wrapped with fear. In this time, God's message is all the more crucial. This message of fear and hope, the message of God's power and human reaction through obedience, the message that our small obedience brings forth God's greatest gifts for the world, are reprisals that repeat time and again and throughout time and space.

In our closed room, we encounter our God in the midst of our hope and fear, just as Mary did, and just as Jesus's disciples did. Through our encounter with God, God takes care of our fear, nourishes our hope, and gives the message in our lips and hearts so that we may cry out God's message to the world that Jesus, who is always with us, is born.

Prayer

Our God, you meet us in our fear. You find us when no one expects great things from us. You are God who leads us and guides us. Even when we cannot fully understand you, let us keep trusting you. Let us sing Mary's song, Hannah's song, and a number of songs sung by your people. Let us remember and honor your people who have practiced mercies in your name. Let us follow their steps, but in our own way, in faithfulness and in mutual relationship with you and all your people. Let us keep our hope in you and rejoice in Jesus, who is the Savior for all your people.

Chapter Four

Christmas Is Only the Beginning

God Sends the Church to the World

AMY VALDEZ BARKER

The Little Drummer Boy

Pa rum pa pum pum...

My mother told this story almost every Christmas growing up. It started with, "Do you remember that cold Christmas Eve at the Menorah hospital, after I had my first baby? Dad had to go so that he could open the church for the Christmas Eve service, and it was just you and me, Amy. The only thing I remember was the song 'Little Drummer Boy,' playing on the radio all night long while I held my newborn baby girl." She always told it as though she expected me to remember that night, as if it was supposed to be a memory etched forever in my mind. This is the image of me as a newborn infant, and my mother, a young immigrant woman, whose husband was a student pastor serving as the church janitor, stuck in a hospital room with low lights and a radio playing softly in the background those haunting unforgettable lyrics, "Come, they told me…pa rum pa pum pum." I don't remember it, but I always remember her telling me the story year after year so it would be cemented in my mind. The beauty of that memory is that it has become a foundation to my identity; it is the story that defines me and the song that reminds me who I am and to whom I belong.

Advent is that foundational story for all of us who follow the Christian faith. It is that time of reminding us who we are and to whom we belong. It is the story of our beginning that points to our future and gives us hope for what is yet to come. Every time I hear "The Little Drummer Boy," I see that image in my mind of a young mother, looking lovingly at her newborn child with all the hope, desires, and unfathomable love that she could ever imagine. It is the song of the messenger signaling to the world that there is something coming, there is something to do and there is an expectation that the world will respond. That is what Advent does. That is what Advent is meant to do.

Messenger and Message

*In those days a decree went out from Emperor
Augustus that all the world should be registered.
This was the first registration and was taken while
Quirinius was governor of Syria. All went to their
own towns to be registered. Joseph also went from the
town of Nazareth in Galilee to Judea, to the city of
David called Bethlehem, because he was descended
from the house and family of David. He went to be
registered with Mary, to whom he was engaged and
who was expecting a child. While they were there, the
time came for her to deliver her child. And she gave
birth to her firstborn son and wrapped him in bands
of cloth, and laid him in a manger, because there was
no place for them in the inn.*

*In that region there were shepherds living in the
fields, keeping watch over their flock by night. Then
an angel of the Lord stood before them, and the
glory of the Lord shone around them, and they were
terrified. But the angel said to them, "Do not be
afraid; for see—I am bringing you good news of great
joy for all the people: to you is born this day in the city
of David a Savior, who is the Messiah, the Lord. This
will be a sign for you: you will find a child wrapped in
bands of cloth and lying in a manger." And suddenly
there was with the angel a multitude of the heavenly
host, praising God and saying,*

> *"Glory to God in the highest heaven,*
> *and on earth peace among those whom he*
> *favors!"*

When the angels had left them and gone into
heaven, the shepherds said to one another, "Let us
go now to Bethlehem and see this thing that has
taken place, which the Lord has made known to
us." So they went with haste and found Mary and
Joseph, and the child lying in the manger. When
they saw this, they made known what had been told
them about this child; and all who heard it were
amazed at what the shepherds told them. But Mary
treasured all these words and pondered them in
her heart. The shepherds returned, glorifying and
praising God for all they had heard and seen, as it
had been told them.

Luke 2:1-20

The story of Jesus's birth as told by the author of Luke is all about the messenger, the message, and the response to the message. It is about the call to action that invites the reader to recognize that this momentous event led to a significant change in the lives of every person involved. From Mary and Joseph to the shepherds in the field to the people who received the news from the shepherds, each person involved was sent a messenger who delivered a message that changed their lives. Just as God had intended, the word spread throughout the land that a new king had been born who would disrupt the powers of this world in order to bring a new kind of power for the world of the future. It was a message that transformed how humanity interacted with the Divine, and it has been shaping the world for more than two thousand years. Throughout this chapter we will examine how God has invited us to do all the good we can through the messenger, the message, and our invitation to participate in God's creation by actively responding.

The Active Response

The authors of the Gospels form a fascinating collection of messengers, each conveying the same message but to different audiences of people, which would draw out a contextually relevant response. For example, scholars remind us that the Gospel of Luke offers the perspective of a non-Jew who sought to tell the message of Jesus in a way that could be understood by those unfamiliar with the Jewish faith. This messenger of the Gospel of Luke took time to carefully chronicle the events that led up to Jesus's birth, giving credibility to the life of the Savior who was sent to transform the world. As a physician, according to Paul (Colossians 4:14), Luke has a keen sense of care for the people who are part of his narrative about Jesus. The author of Luke meticulously weaves an image of the humanity of Jesus throughout the Gospel. At the same time, he illustrates where Jesus came from as he ties Jesus's lineage back to his ancestral connections with David as the "chosen one." Additionally the actions highlighted throughout Luke portray Jesus as one who does not allow the weaknesses of humanity, like power and greed, to keep him from fulfilling his call as both the messenger and the message that comes from God.

This idea of messenger to message to active response appears throughout the biblical text, beyond the Gospels. Each time you open the Bible, you will find some story of messengers who were called forth by God to deliver some message to God's creation that is intended to bring them back into alignment with God. From Abraham and Isaac to David and Goliath, to Ruth and Naomi or even Esther, there is a messenger in each story, a message that God needs delivered to God's creation and an invitation to action that is an expected response from God's people. The author of Luke most frequently puts the Holy Spirit as the central influencer in the Jesus narrative.

Holy Spirit as Messenger Then and Now

Messengers go before the action. Even in the Genesis story, the Spirit of God was hovering over the waters before the Creator spoke the words bringing light and darkness into the world. Awaiting instructions, the Spirit of God took the message of God and put it into action. It is a beautiful testament to the way the world is delicately designed, often awaiting a catalyst to put things in motion. Without breath there is no life. *Ruach* is the Hebrew word for breath and is found in the Old Testament at the creation of humanity. In Job 33:4 Elihu presses Job, reminding him of the breath of God that gives life. This word is also used to mean "spirit." And in both the Psalms and the Book of Samuel, the authors speak to the presence and then absence of the Spirit when sin is present, and goodness seems absent. John Wesley views the Spirit as both instigator and sustainer of the good that is inherently a part of us as the created ones. The Holy Spirit goes before us, within us, and beyond us as the messenger, the message, and the catalyst for the actions given to us by the will of God.

The passage in Luke clearly gives us a glimpse of the power of the Holy Spirit as the angel says to Mary, "The Holy Spirit will come on you, and the power of the Most High will overshadow you. So the holy one to be born will be called the Son of God" (Luke 1:35 NIV). This messenger/instigator/catalyst caused the movement that followed the birth of Jesus into the world as *ruach* when hope was needed for all.

Messenger moments where the Holy Spirit is at work are all around us. In many ways, these dissenters claim their wisdom comes from the Holy Spirit calling for change in the world. The biblical prophets were God's messengers who were sometimes accepted, but more often rejected because the message was counter to the culture and often met resistance from the powers of that time and those places. Standing against the norm took bravery and confidence and more important, trust that the Holy Spirit was with them, guiding them, inspiring them, and reminding them that this is God's greater intention for the world. The more recent heroes who have been messengers through the power of the Holy Spirit have been leaders such as Mother Teresa, Martin Luther King Jr., and even missionaries, like E. Stanley Jones. These leaders opened their hearts and minds to submit to the power of God's Spirit in their lives, even to the point of death. In their biographies, we read that each one of them battled their egocentric nature, allowing themselves to be vessels for the work of the Spirit.

Jesus, in Mark 13:8-11, gives us an example of how important it is for us to allow the Spirit to deliver the message that is formed and inspired by God and needed for a particular group of people to hear.

> *"Nation will rise against nation, and kingdom against kingdom. There will be earthquakes in various places, and famines. These are the beginning of birth pains.*
>
> *"You must be on your guard. You will be handed over to the local councils and flogged in the synagogues. On account of me you will stand before governors and kings as witnesses to them. And the gospel must first be preached to all nations. Whenever you are arrested and brought to trial, do not worry beforehand about what to say. Just say whatever is given you at the time, for it is not you speaking, but the Holy Spirit." (NIV)*

Mother Teresa lived among the poorest of the poor, giving up all the treasures of the world to ensure that the gospel message was delivered through the power of the Holy Spirit. Martin Luther King Jr. faced anger, hatred, and threats from those who wanted to keep segregation alive in the South and those who wanted it ended by any means possible. King was "handed over" and faced the "governors and the kings" of his time. Had it not been for the power of the Holy Spirit through the deep and unwavering faith he had in his Christian understanding of the world, he would have given in to the pressures of the human condition, allowing the evils of segregation to continue to torment people of color. As Wesley noted, it is the "immediate cause of all holiness in us…leading us in our actions, purifying and sanctifying our souls and our bodies, to a full and eternal enjoyment of God."[1] Without this unwavering faith in the power of the Holy Spirit, God's chosen messengers of our recent history may not have been able to fulfill the transformative vision God had given them for the bettering of a broken world.

The messenger prepares the way for the message. However, without a message, the action would never take place.

The Message Is Jesus

It was less than two months from my thirtieth birthday when my son was born. He was a healthy seven-pound baby who surpassed his sister's birth height and weight by a few centimeters and a couple of ounces. The day he was born was the day before I was scheduled to conduct a friend's wedding. My husband, my daughter, and I were all members of the wedding party, and everyone was excited to be a part of this holy matrimony. However, I warned the couple early in the counseling process that the doctor had given me a due date close to their wedding date. And so, we made contingency plans, just in case. After Tré was born and the drugs started to wear off, my husband looked at me with a question in his eyes. It was the night of the rehearsal, and both baby and I were groggy and tired from all the work of bringing him into the world. I wasn't in any shape to have guests, even my husband and sweet little girl, so I encouraged them to go to the wedding rehearsal and celebrate with our friend in preparation for the wedding the next day. Tré and I would gladly sleep the night away. But after they left and the quietness of the hospital room warmly enfolded me, I didn't sleep. Instead, my mind drifted to thoughts of my mother the night I was born, holding me and listening to the "pa rum pa pum pum" of the little drummer boy echoing in her room. I remember being overwhelmed by the beauty and wonder of the little baby boy sweetly sleeping—in my arms. (There is nothing quite like that feeling in all the world.) Best of all, in that moment, I realized my little bundle of joy was a sweet message of love from God, the Creator, for me, the created one.

Everything about Advent points to the Message, Jesus. When you stare into the face of a newborn child, it is difficult to ignore the innocence and purity in this new human soul. With every coo and cry, there is a message being conveyed that is difficult to understand until you have spent enough time together. Words are unnecessary in these early moments of bonding; it is just a heightened sensitivity that comes with paying attention to someone else's needs besides your own. They are messages without words, yet so full of meaning. The message can only be revealed when the receiver is ready to listen.

There was a story I heard many years ago that intrigued me as I wondered about children being the message from God. I discovered that it may have originally been a story told in the book *Chicken Soup for the Soul*. It was about a little four-year-old girl named Sachi who wanted to be left alone with her newborn baby brother. Curious about this request, the parents agreed, but stayed just on the other side of the door, out of sight, but within earshot. They heard Sachi go up to her baby brother and get as close as she could to him and quietly whisper, "Can you tell me what God feels like? I'm starting to forget."

As with a new life, when one receives a brand-new message, there is much excitement, hope, anticipation, and possibility. But as we get further from the initial revelation of the message, our memories begin to fade, and that exciting new moment gets replaced with everyday busyness and that message disappears into the background of our minds. Even though it is in the background, many of us, with little effort, can recall those important moments when the message of life, through our children's births, our marriages, or other meaningful spiritual events, can be brought forward in our memories and treasured as if they just happened yesterday. That is the gift of the everlasting message of Jesus Christ, who sent the Holy Spirit to be with us as an ever-present partner in communion with humanity, helping us recall the message of grace.

I treasured and still treasure every moment I have with both my children. They are gifts of life ripe with possibilities. Their lives continue to be a love letter between me and God, a constant reminder at how beautiful and how fragile life is. Jesus as the love letter to humanity from the Creator is the foundation of our Christian identity. Messages convey meaning and intention. The message of Jesus, the Christ child, conveys the intention God has for all of God's creation through the Incarnation. When we remember this message each year at Advent, we are reminded about the foundation of our faith. We are invited to hold on to the promise of eternal life through God's love for us.

John Wesley's "Plain Account of Christian Perfection" also helps bring meaning to the message of Jesus in a contemporary way. He writes, "It is that habitual disposition of soul which, in the sacred writings, is termed holiness; and which directly implies, being cleansed from sin 'from all filthiness both of flesh and spirit;' and, by consequence, being endued with those virtues which were in Christ Jesus being so 'renewed in the image of our mind,' as to be 'perfect as our Father in heaven is perfect'" (PCP, 5:203). He goes on to make the case that the entire message of Jesus, the risen Christ, can be wrapped up in the gift of *love*. From the sermon titled "The *Circumcision of the Heart*," he quotes:

> "Love is the fulfilling of the law, the end of the commandment." It is not only the first and great command, but all the commandments in one. "Whatsoever things are just, whatsoever things are pure, if there be any virtue, if there be any praise," they are all comprised in one word, love. In this is perfection, and glory, and happiness; the royal

law of heaven and earth is this, 'Thou shall love the Lord thy God with all thy heart, and with all thy soul, and with all thy mind, and with all thy strength." The one perfect good shall be your one ultimate end. (SCH)

Jesus is the message of love. God's unfathomable love for us is so deep that it took God's presence on earth for humanity to begin to understand the perfect nature of the Creator, a nature so deeply engulfed in love that there are very few other meanings or stories behind this message. The heart of God's message through Jesus is love. That resonates deeply with me. Whenever I look at my children, the overwhelming message that returns to me is love. There is nothing on earth that I would do for my children that is too great to convey my deep love for them. The actions I have taken since they were born are often fraught with questions about how it will affect their lives. Love for my family pulses heavily through my veins. If this is but a tiny drop of the magnitude of love God has for us, then I can see how the message of Christian love has survived through the centuries. Dr. Dana Robert points to the miraculous nature of this message enduring the test of time in her book *Christian Mission: How Christianity Became a World Religion*. She writes, "Because of its embodiment in human cultures—an idea that theologians refer to as 'incarnation'—the Christian message has outlasted clans and tribes, nations and empires, monarchies, democracies, and military dictatorships. When a handful of Jesus' Jewish followers reached out to non-Jews in the Roman empire, they unknowingly set their faith on the path toward becoming a world religion."[2] The incarnational message of Jesus, understood to be the risen Christ, is no less than a miracle, enduring the millennia, finding its way as seeds germinating the human heart. Jesus is the message of love.

A Message That Leads to Action

The Christmas Eve Service of 2006 will join the vault of memories that are transformative for me and my children. My son, Tré, was less than two months old at the time. My colleague, Jenny Seylar, the associate pastor at Coralville UMC, was like an angel for me during those first few months of Tré's life. She and I, led by the Holy Spirit, made the decision to rewrite the birth story of Jesus from the perspectives of Mary and the innkeeper's wife. In that time and place, women cared for women, especially during the childbirth process.

Jenny and I crafted the reflection from the eyes of a new mother and the heart of a caring soul who was privy to the birth of the Savior of the world. We dressed up as we imagined Mary and the innkeeper's wife would have dressed in the desert lands of Bethlehem. We talked about the weary experience of travelers coming into the town to fulfill their civic duties. Playing the part of Mary, I confessed to the heartaches and struggles that came with being a woman giving birth in that time in a dirty stable with a stranger, wondering if I would live to see the child who grew inside me. Jenny, playing the innkeeper's wife, reflected on this strange couple who came with no place to go except the barn her husband had offered them in the middle of the night. Both of our monologues revealed the very human nature of the people surrounding the Christ child on that first symbolic night of the Christian faith. To add to the reality of the experience, about halfway through the second service, my "baby Jesus" had enough. In the middle of my monologue, he started to fuss, and the sweet little whimpers grew into a full-blown cry. Because I wasn't able to talk over my infant's voice, my angel Jenny came in and picked him up, dancing with him and soothing him in the way only an experienced mother could, giving me a momentary reprieve, which is what I needed to finish the words that were still on my tongue as I recalled the experience of Mary. For so many that Christmas Eve, it was a new rendition of the Christmas story, touching the hearts of the hundreds who had made their way out that evening. Our reflections reminded those who had come to worship that the people who were there when Jesus was born were human, full of angst, full of emotions, completely unprepared for how this message of love would change the world. Messages matter, and God's love turned this message into action.

Our Methodist Theology of Action

Usually, messages have a purpose. The message God sent through Jesus, the Son of God, had a very distinctive call to action. The Christmas message is not merely a passive story for people to feel good about the moment, although many in our Christian communities today act as if that is the sole and whole purpose of Advent. This is a message to the people then as it is to us today with a real purpose to inspire humanity and implore us to see that our actions need to change. If we are to truly respond to the call that God has placed in each person at creation, then we would need to act differently, think differently, and live differently. It was clear that humanity, through our sinfulness, failed to stay on the path God had intended. However, this call to action is not offered to earn a position with God. God did not desire for the action to be understood as the way to get the seat at the right hand of the Father. For those of us who are ambitious, our Western culture teaches us that there is an expectation for earning your way into God's good graces. It tells us that if you fail to be good, those good graces can be taken away. This is not true of the Methodist theology of faith in action.

Methodists do not believe that we can earn our way to heaven by doing good deeds. We do not advocate for a transactional relationship with God. We do not believe that each good decision, good word, or good action will result in God loving us more. This is not part of our DNA, even though there are many faith traditions that currently and historically offer this kind of understanding of God. Because it is so common, it is easy to fall into this misunderstanding as well. Our contemporary cultures have taught us that this transactional nature is part of our being. We have even used snippets from the Bible to back up our rationale for these transactions in life. If you scratch my back, I will scratch yours. Many point to Leviticus 24:19-22, which states, "Anyone who injures their neighbor is to be injured in the same manner: fracture for fracture, eye for eye, tooth for tooth. The one who has inflicted the injury must suffer the same injury. Whoever kills an animal must make restitution, but whoever kills a human being is to be put to death. You are to have the same law for the foreigner and the native-born. I am the Lord your God" (NIV). We often take this scripture and use it to our advantage when we have been wronged or someone we know has been wronged. But if we are the ones who caused harm, this passage can be challenging. Our nature is to turn to these passages and justify our transactional actions as we neglect and often even forget the message that has come through the birth of the chosen One.

But as Christians who follow the Wesleyan understanding of our faith, we believe in the transforming nature of God's love through grace that leads us to live out our lives fully under the gift of love we experience through Jesus Christ. In other words, the actions we offer stem from the overwhelming power of love. Not because we expect anything in return. Our gift of salvation has already been given to us, so our actions stem out of our love for all of God's creation and all of God's world. Therefore, Methodists are actively engaged in transforming the world through actions that are often for the greater good. Think about all the places where the Methodist movement has improved communities through their actions. Methodist movements worldwide have often been at the forefront of healing the broken world through education, through hospitals and clinics, and through community centers and institutions oriented toward grace, hope, and love that can be experienced in real and tangible ways. Methodists across the world have stepped into community-serving roles because they are living under the lordship of Jesus Christ as faithful disciples who are covered in amazing grace. Amazing grace actions are the heart of the call of those who follow the Wesleyan way.

The Gift of Amazing Grace Actions

In all the places I have had the privilege of traveling throughout the world, I have found amazing grace actions at work through the people called Methodist. I have been blessed by these stories of amazing grace actions, stories that have transformed communities, stories of dedicated Christians living within the covenant of the Wesleyan understanding of faith. There is a beautiful network of nearly forty million Methodists in over 138 different countries around the world who have taken the message of Jesus to offer us these amazing grace stories and use their lives to live as transformed people. They serve as missionaries, deaconesses, deacons, and elders in the Methodist systems. They serve as lay leaders who start social services, offer medical support, offer sacred safe spaces in the midst of challenging circumstances throughout the world. They lean in to hard situations, fighting powerful political leaders, and some have died as a result of doing what they knew God had called them to do. These and so many others are passionate people seeking to do all the good they can in all the places they can. It's actions that come out of a heart that has been fully oriented toward God and wholly transformed by love.

Here are a few stories of these amazing grace actions that have happened around the world.

I met Miracle Osman on the Connectional Table of The United Methodist Church. She was a young adult from Malawi who had been invited to serve as a board member in this connection. Miracle felt God's call to serve and ended up being selected to serve as a Global Mission Fellow for two years. In that time, she was sent to the Philippines to serve among the Lumad tribe in the southern islands of the Philippines, called Mindanao. During her service, she was responsible for working with the children, teaching them English and encouraging them through Bible stories and stories of hope. As a woman from Malawi, Miracle may have been one of the first Africans these children had ever met. During her time there, new political leadership came into place and Miracle plus two other young leaders, Tawanda Chandiwana and Adam Shaw (UM News Service), who had been serving with her in mission, were being tracked, monitored, and even harassed. Tawanda was detained, and Miracle's passport was confiscated. Adam was also being questioned. It was a treacherous endeavor for these young people, who were in a foreign land, responding to God's call on their lives. And yet, they knew Christ's message to do all the good they could would lead them into unknown places. Through the efforts of the entire Methodist connection, a cry to "Let them leave!" was sent out through social media, and more than sixteen thousand people in fewer than twenty-four hours had signed the petition to the Philippine government, requesting the release of the three young leaders who had been serving God faithfully and bringing light to the injustices faced by the people in those communities. Their amazing grace actions provided a witness for how God could transform people's hearts and minds anywhere in the world. They inspired others to go and serve in God's name. Their story illustrates how God could move governments through the power of the Holy Spirit connection, doing all the good they can.

Another story of amazing grace actions comes from a local church near my present community. I had the great gift to serve in youth ministry in this congregation. There were so many wonderful and amazing leaders who would volunteer their time, energy, and resources to do all the good they could in their church and in their community. My most memorable amazing grace action came in the form of a dear friend named Deana Jones. She was always oriented toward helping everyone in her life, and one year I was the beneficiary of that good help. I had been on a senior high ski trip that January, and unfortunately, I was one of the lucky ones who, without being aware of it, went down a black diamond ski run. Black diamonds are marked as being the most challenging slopes on a mountain and are reserved for the most experienced skiers. They are not for novice, overly confident wannabe experts like me. This unfortunate turn led me to tumble down the hill and tear every ligament possible in my knee. Looking back, it was somewhat amusing that the congregation had prayed for the youth to return safely but it was the youth minister who was injured. It was a terribly painful injury that led to two surgeries and months of physical therapy. But when my husband was not going to be able to help me on the day of the surgery due to other pressing obligations, Deana stepped up and helped out. She took me back to her home after the outpatient surgery and waited on me hand and foot, ensuring that my wounds were tended, the medicine was delivered at just the right times, and I was as comfortable as I could be coming out of recovery. Her amazing grace actions were humbling to a person like me. I always saw myself as the one who served others. This time, I was in need of the support and care, and my friend took immediate action and responded with overwhelming love and grace. That moment reminded me that the victim in the parable of the good Samaritan was the recipient of the amazing grace action. And both the good Samaritan and the man who had needed his help were transformed because of those actions. They were born of the work of the Spirit, and their response was due to God's great work through the message of Jesus in the world.

Wesley wrote in his sermon "The First Fruits of the Spirit" about how those who have received the message and own the message of Christ Jesus live life differently, and because of that transformation in their lives, each and every action is in line with the Spirit.

> They now "walk after the Spirit," both in their
> hearts and lives. They are taught of him to love

God and their neighbour, with a love which is as
"a well of water, springing up into everlasting life."
And by him they are led into every holy desire,
into every divine and heavenly temper, till every
thought which arises in their heart is holiness unto
the Lord.

I love this image of a "well of water, springing into everlasting life," because it reminds me of the many faithful people in my life who have been that "well of water" for me in a number of ways. Their actions have illustrated how they "walk after the Spirit" in all that they do and how they seek that love of all of God's creation in every step they take. It is a gift of the Spirit that overwhelms my soul when I have the opportunity to walk under the spring of holy waters that pour from their souls. Each of us has those people in our lives. They are the people who are not just the unsung heroes like Miracle whose actions and experiences seem far from our own, but they are also the people who are in our own homes, our own families, and even in our own faith communities. They are the people who take the time to know their neighbors in order to offer hope. They are the people who check in on one another, just in case someone has been all alone. They are the people who volunteer at hospitals, schools, sports clubs, civic organizations, wanting to offer kindness and hope so that their community members know they are not alone. Some of these people do it because they are fully aware of the message of Jesus that has been delivered into their hearts and souls and has led them to "walk after the Spirit." Others are doing it before they are even fully aware of the goodness that resides in them through the power of the Spirit as the gift of prevenient grace. God's message is in our hearts and souls, and God uses the power of the Spirit to bring it to the forefront of our hearts and minds.

Perfected in Love

I used to teach sessions about what it meant to be striving toward "Christian perfection." And inevitably, participants would have a strong defensive response toward this idea of "Christian perfection." Western culture has taken and distorted this idea of a "perfect love" into an idealistic image that leaves little to no room for error. We have images of models, perfectly air-brushed images of women and men that are far from their real looks. They have monopolized the culture by adding stories of "perfect romances," in movies, TV shows, and music videos that do not really capture the messiness of relationships. Because of this, we have bent the term "perfection" and further ostracized people by adding the word "Christian" in front of it as a way to make people believe that once you become a Christian, you have to live life perfectly, without mistakes, without sin, without failing anyone or failing in anything. This is far from the way "Christian perfection" was being interpreted in Wesley's day. Being "perfected in love," as Wesley puts it, means that our actions are primarily oriented toward the agape love God planted in our hearts at the beginning of Creation. But it doesn't mean that it doesn't take our action and our repentance for us to see this gift of love God has instilled in our hearts. God has still given us the response-ability to recognize God's actions in our lives and in our world.

In his sermon "The Scripture Way of Salvation," Wesley focuses in on Ephesians 2:8 and speaks to how the message of Jesus brought us to a salvific response that moves our hearts toward love. The love of God and the love of neighbor is the most beautiful and perfect way we can live our lives because of what God has done through his Son, Jesus, the risen Christ.

Wesley writes:

> "But what is that faith whereby we are sanctified,—saved from sin, and perfected in love." It is a divine evidence and conviction, first, that God hath promised it in the holy Scripture. Till we are thoroughly satisfied of this, therein no moving one step further. And one would imagine there needed not one word more to satisfy a reasonable man of this, than the ancient promise, "Then will I circumcise thy heart, and the heart of thy seed, to love the Lord thy God with all thy heart, and with all thy soul, and with all thy mind." How clearly does this express the being perfected in love! —how strongly imply the being saved from all sin! For as long as love takes up the whole heart, what room is there for sin therein? (SSWS, 2:14)

Perfected in love is God's action in us through the power of Jesus, the risen Christ. Perfected in love is the gift of salvation "from all sin! For as long as love takes up the whole heart, what room is there for sin therein?" All those images of perfection and ideologies around what our human expectation of perfection is and what God's expectation of perfection is have been disrupted by the Creator. Wesley understood that our human understanding was limited, but God's understanding was limitless. At the end of the day, the everyday actions of those of us who have leaned into being "perfected in love" are the necessary movements that continue to offer healing and hope in a broken world. If it were not for our continual movement toward this desire for living into that perfect love, the world would be more broken than it has ever been. But through the miracle of Jesus, the message in action through the power of the Holy Spirit in the world today, we have hope. We can see visions of a better future, where we are both actors in the transformation and recipients of the transformation.

Christian perfection is both a moment and a process. It is the moment of birth where a new human being is brought into the world. The moment of birth when the soul enters the body. Christian perfection is the moment when we are awakened from our "sleeping state," and moved into a justified state because we have faith. These are the moments we can point to that are marked by a specific time. For many, it is the Advent moment that is remembered, recalled, and recognized each year where we welcome the Creator into the world through the infant child.

But Christian perfection is also a process that is a constant movement of thoughts, ideas, and practices that become manifested in action. It's the risks that people take when they deny themselves and make sacrifices for others. They are both big actions and small actions. Actions that are decisions like the decision Miracle and the missionaries in the Philippines made to respond to God's love in their hearts by risking their lives to share love with the children. Actions that are like what my friend Deana did for me as a self-denying moment in order to offer God's love and grace to a wounded and ill friend. These are the actions that illustrate the process of Christian perfection swelling in the Christ-oriented heart.

Advent: The Messenger— the Message—The Action

Every year we are told the story of the birth of Jesus as a reminder of who we are and to whom we belong. Like my mother recalling the story of my birthday, Christians around the world recall the moment that the perfected love of God entered the world through God's only begotten Son. It is the story that grounds our identity in a Creator God who deeply cared for all of God's creation. This identity as Christian people is our defining WHY our presence in the world matters. It is the practice time we need as we move back into the world, sharing God's love and God's grace with everyone we meet. Christmas is only the beginning.

"Hark! The Herald Angels Sing" is the song of the messenger, the song that carries forth the message of Jesus as the whole embodiment of love that is the foundation of the Christian faith.

Charles Wesley is the original author of the lyrics of this hymn, but it was through the years edited by John and their colleague George Whitefield. As yet another form taken by the messenger, this song uplifts the message of Jesus as the celebrated One in whom we all, as Christians, plant our identity. Recall how the words in this hymn imprint upon us a theological understanding of God incarnate through the Son. Jesus is the message—Jesus calls us all to action. Jesus through the Spirit dwells in us as the living witness to the actions in our lives. Every good and faithful action is in response to this indwelling of God within each person. It is the good news of life! This is the good news that should be pronounced from the mountains, magnified across the oceans, and multiplied as generously as the sands in the desert. Of course, all the angels are singing! Wouldn't you also be singing about the message that is this newborn King?

But the message doesn't just end with the good news; it is an invitation to constantly be turning to God as the Creator, who invites us to be full participants in God's creation. The message doesn't just leave us with the momentary celebration but pushes us toward the journey with the Holy Spirit. Through the beauty of the message, and the gift of the Holy Spirit, we move into the world renewed.

Prayer

Amazing and holy Creator God, who has seen the beginning and understands the end, the One who is omnipresent with us, sending us the power of the Holy Spirit through the messenger and the message, we are overwhelmed by your omnipotent grace. We give thanks for each magnificent moment you have painted on the canvas of life, seeing the vision of humanity before the seed had ever been planted. We give thanks for the miracles that happen throughout our lives that open our eyes to the wonder of your Creation. We know you use these moments through your gifts to constantly transform all things toward mission in the world. Each and every action toward good brings us that much closer to your love and grace. We honor you, delight in you, and seek to respond faithfully to you as we live under your gift of salvation.

Take our actions, our words, our good deeds, and use them all to your glory. Help us be vessels of your transforming power as you bring healing to the brokenness in our world. We love you, God, and we are forever changed by your Son, whose message we remember this Advent season and whose Spirit we will join as we go about doing all the good we can in the world you have made.

This, O Holy Creator, and so much more, we offer to YOU!

AMEN!

Notes

Chapter 1

1   From *The Book of Discipline of The United Methodist Church*, 2016. Copyright © 2016 by The United Methodist Publishing House; ¶ 104, page 78. Used by permission.

2   Thomas R. Albin, "An Empirical Study of Early Methodist Spirituality," *Wesleyan Theology Today: A Bicentennial Theological Consultation,* edited by Theodore Runyon, 277-78 (Nashville: Kingswood Books, 1985).

3   Mary McLeod Bethune, "Spiritual Autobiography," in *Bethune, Building a Better World: Essays and Selected Documents*, ed. Audrey Thomas McCluskey and Elaine M. Smith (Bloomington: Indiana University Press, 2001), 53.

4   Mary McLeod Bethune, quoted in Judith Weisenfeld and Richard Newman, eds., *This Far by Faith: Readings in African-American Women's Religious Biography* (New York: Routledge, 1996), 137.

Chapter 2

1   John Calvin, *Commentary on the Psalms: 1–35* (Algenmunster: Jazzybee Verlag, 2012), author's preface.

2   Martin Heidegger, "Letter on Humanism," in *Heidegger: Basic Writings*, ed. David Farrell Krell (New York: Harper & Row, 1977), 193.

3   Emily Brontë, *Wuthering Heights* (London: Penguin Books, 2003), 175.

4   Gregory of Nazianzus, "Letters (Division I)," trans. Charles Gordon Browne and James Edward Swallow, in *Nicene and Post-Nicene Fathers*, vol. 7, ed. Philip Schaff and Henry Wace (Buffalo, NY: Christian Literature, 1894). Revised and edited for New Advent by Kevin Knight, http://www.newadvent.org/fathers/3103a.htm.

5   Grégoire de Nazianze, Oration 1, 5, in Discours 1–3, ed. J. Bernardi (1978, 2006).

6   Charles Wesley, *Hymns and Sacred Poems* (1740), 66.

Chapter 3

1   The image may be found at the Philadelphia Museum of Art or its website (www.philamuseum.org).

2   Fred B. Craddock, *Luke: Interpretation: A Bible Commentary for Teaching and Preaching* (Louisville: Westminster John Knox Press, 2009), 30.

3   Thomas N. Ivey, ed., *Southern Methodist Handbook 1916* (Nashville: Publishing House M. E. Church, South; Smith & Lamar, agents, 1916).

Chapter 4

1   *The Letters of the Rev. John Wesley, A.M.*, ed. John Telford (London: Epworth, 1931), 3:9.

2   Dana L. Robert, *Christian Mission: How Christianity Became a World Religion,* Wiley-Blackwell Brief Histories of Religion (West Sussex, UK: Wiley-Blackwell, 2009), loc. 103 of 2819, Kindle.